at to do when someone dies

By the same author

Getting a Job in America

Getting a Job Abroad

howtobooks

Send for a free copy of the latest catalogue to:
How To Books
Spring Hill House
Spring Hill Road, Begbroke
Oxford OX5 1RX, United Kingdom
email: info@howtobooks.co.uk
http://www.howtobooks.co.uk

What to do when someone dies

DEALING WITH DEATH, FUNERALS, WILLS AND BEREAVEMENT

A practical guide

ROGER JONES

howto books

Published by How To Books Ltd,
Spring Hill House,
Spring Hill Road, Begbroke
Oxford OX5 1RX, United Kingdom.
Tel: (01865) 375794. Fax: (01865) 379162.
email: info@howtobooks.co.uk
http://www.howtobooks.co.uk

British Library Cataloguing in Publication Data
A catalogue record for this book is available from the British Library

Cover design by Baseline Arts Ltd, Oxford
Produced for How To Books by Deer Park Productions, Tavistock
Typeset by TW Typesetting, Plymouth, Devon
Printed and bound by The Cromwell Press, Trowbridge, Wiltshire.

NOTE: The material contained in this book is set out in good faith for general guidance and no liability can be accepted for loss or expense incurred as a result of relying in particular circumstances on statements made in the book. The laws and regulations are complex and liable to change, and readers should check the current position with the relevant authorities before making personal arrangements.

Contents

List of Figures

Preface

'When my father died, we didn't have a clue what to do,' a neighbour confessed to me recently. I wonder how many others have found themselves in a similar predicament when a close relative or friend has died.

A death is – mercifully – no longer the frequent occurrence it was in Victorian times. As a consequence people tend to overlook it. We are more likely to make plans for how we will spend our winnings in the lottery (an unlikely event) rather than plan ahead for our decease (which is a certainty).

There is another problem. Death has become a taboo topic that we shy away from discussing. Even when there a signs that a death is imminent, we want to dismiss it from our minds, and so find ourselves totally unprepared to deal with it when it happens.

Most deaths these days occur after people have completed their three score years and ten and are largely predictable. But others occur unexpectedly – the result perhaps of a natural disaster, an accident or a sudden illness. If it is the death of a young person, the shock is all the greater.

Who should take charge when someone dies? Who needs to be informed of the death? What do you do with the body?

How do you set about arranging a funeral? Who pays for it? What role does the undertaker play? What happens to the deceased's property and other assets? Is a solicitor needed to administer the will?

You may know the answers to some of these questions, but may have only a hazy notion of how to cope with some of the other matters. Eventually you will find out through trial and error, but how much better it would be if you have a clear idea of what to expect right from the start. This would not only make the whole process less painful and traumatic, but enable you to make decisions with greater confidence.

I have written this book in order to clear a path through the haze, not because I take pleasure in writing on gloomy topics but because I believe people may find dealing with a death less intimidating if they have some practical guidelines to work to.

Having experienced bereavement more than once myself I am aware of the problems and dilemmas one can be faced with. I therefore felt it might be helpful to share my experiences with others who suddenly find themselves in a similar situation.

I do not claim that the book deals with every eventuality, but I hope it will steer you in the right direction and alert you of the matters you need to attend to. If you require further information and help, you will find the addresses and websites of agencies and organisations with plenty of experience in assisting people in their time of need.

Finally, I hope I will not be accused of insensitivity if I urge those who are aware their days are numbered to read this book as well – particularly the first chapter. You may feel you are tempting fate by contemplating your own death, but by making suitable preparations for your decease, you will render your passing less painful and traumatic for those who survive you.

Roger Jones

1

Anticipating the End

My first chapter is addressed not to the recently bereaved, but to anyone who is going to die, which – in effect – means each one of us. This may seem a strange way to begin a book on how to deal with death and its aftermath, but since we are all mortal it seems logical to think ahead and prepare for our eventual demise.

Happily, thanks largely to improvements in health, most of us – over 90 per cent in the Western world – can expect to live until 65 or beyond. That does not mean, however, that we can dismiss the prospect of death from our minds entirely. An accident, a natural disaster or a sudden epidemic, for example, could befall anybody, and I can think of several instances of young people who have died tragically while still in their teens or twenties.

While it is perhaps too much to expect young people of this age to plan for their departure from this world, others of slightly more mature years should definitely give this matter some thought, especially if they have dependants or have started to accumulate assets.

Death may signify the end for the person concerned, but not for those who have to deal with the consequences of a death. At a time when they are suffering grief and shock, they will have to busy themselves registering your death, arranging your funeral, settling outstanding bills, notifying seemingly countless organisations from the telephone company to the tax office, disposing of your assets – and that is only the start.

Attending to the aftermath of a death can be a time-consuming, frustrating, tiresome and traumatic affair. That is why it behoves all of us to put our affairs in order before we pass on, rather than leave a legacy of chaos and confusion for others to sort out.

YOUR RESPONSIBILITIES TO OTHERS

Your friends and relations may well feel awkward about bringing up the matter of your death with you even though they know your days are numbered. This awkwardness is partly engendered by a fear of upsetting you; but it also has something to do with the fact that death tends to be a taboo subject in polite circles.

It shouldn't be. If you start to discuss death and its implications well before it occurs, the event is likely to be far less devastating for those concerned. It is particularly important to address the practicalities of your death, and to spare others embarrassment it is up to you personally to initiate the discussion and follow it up with appropriate action – such as making a will.

In addition to making a will, it is important to ensure that you keep proper records of your assets and liabilities – car, house, investments, mortgage, loans, etc – so that your executors will know precisely what they are. This is particularly important if you live alone and have nobody to confide in on a day-to-day basis. Relevant documents need to be filed away carefully and interested parties informed of where they are kept.

You also need to leave instructions regarding your funeral arrangements, the addresses of people to contact after your death, your doctor's details, and so on. You might care to obtain from Age Concern their useful eight-page form entitled *Instructions for my Next-of-Kin and Executors upon my Death* and fill it in, or compile your own list using the checklist at the end of this chapter.

This is a matter that people of any age should attend to, rather than wait until they are pushing 90. In several of the major disasters of the current millennium, such as the attack on the World Trade Centre in New York, the tsunami in the Indian Ocean and the earthquake in Kashmir, many of the victims were relatively young. I hope I have made my point!

In view of the risk of dying when you are away from home, it makes sense to leave contact addresses or telephone numbers with those close to you in case of emergencies and also carry details of your next of kin around with you. There is a space for this information in your passport, or you could carry a next of kin card issued by Advice Now or the charity Next of Kin International.

WHO'S IN CHARGE WHEN I DIE?

The short answer is your next of kin and the executor(s) of your will. But complications can arise, especially if you have no will and you have no close relations.

Your next of kin

In the case of those under the age of 18, your parents or guardian will automatically take charge of your affairs if you should die. For those aged 18 or over, it would be your married spouse and/or closest blood relations (parents, siblings, children, etc). However, if your closest relations live on the other side of the world or you have little contact with them, you may prefer to nominate someone else to be your next of kin, such as a close friend or an unmarried partner. You should inform your relations and others with whom you have dealings (doctors, legal advisers, banks, etc) of these arrangements and carry details of your next of kin around with you.

The responsibilities of your next of kin will include:

◆ registering your death

◆ informing relations, friends and other interested parties that you have died

◆ organising the funeral.

Your executor

This is the person who is responsible for administering your will – which involves gathering together your assets, paying any bills and distributing any surplus. It is not necessary to appoint a solicitor as your executor, though this is often done. Bear in mind that if you appoint a solicitor or a bank as your executor there will be fees to pay or a charge based on the value of your estate.

If the will is relatively straightforward lay people aged 18 and over can be appointed to administer your will, and it is up to them whether they decide to employ a solicitor to do some or all of the job. You may appoint up to four executors; a minimum of two is recommended in case one of them dies or is unable to carry out the task. They really ought to be people who are likely to survive you and can be trusted to deal with your affairs comptently and in a business-like fashion.

If you do not make a will, there will not be any executor, and your next of kin will have the task of sorting out your affairs.

WHY SHOULD I BOTHER TO MAKE A WILL?

You may consider yourself to be as poor as the proverbial church mouse, but the chances are you have some assets. By making a will you will ensure that any assets left over when bills have been paid are allocated in accordance with your wishes. It will also make life much easier for those who survive you.

It is worth emphasising that verbal instructions have no legal standing and you need to make a written will in order to ensure that your wishes are carried out.

WILLS MUST BE WRITTEN DOWN

My late mother frequently explained in detail to me how she wanted her assets to be distributed. She seemed to take the view that making a will was unnecessary provided everyone was aware of her wishes. I was reluctant to force the issue, but when she turned 80, I decided I had to take the bull by the horns. I pointed out that unless she left her instructions in written form and had them witnessed, her property and assets would have to be sold and might not be distributed as she would have wished. The penny dropped and a week later she went to see a solicitor about making her will.

If you die without having made a will you will be regarded as having died intestate, which means that your estate will be distributed to your living relatives according to criteria laid down by law, regardless of your real intentions. If you have no living relative it goes to the Crown. (See Figure 1: Rules of Intestacy.)

At what age should you make a will? Legally anyone aged 18 or over may do so and so may members of the armed forces on active service who are under the age of 18. (In Scottish law the minimum age is 12.) In practice very few people in their teens or twenties will bother, and if they possess very few assets, they may feel there is little point. However, once you

Flowchart of the Rules of Intestacy

A ROUGH GUIDE TO WHERE YOUR MONEY GOES IF YOU DIE WITHOUT MAKING A WILL

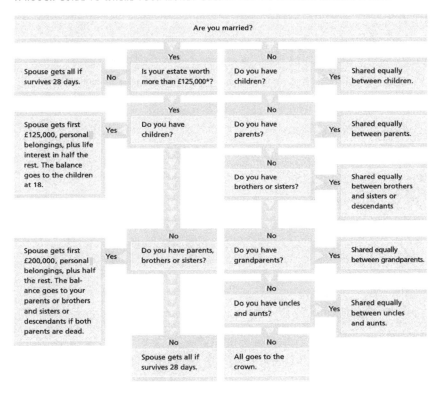

Figure 1. Rules of intestacy.
Scottish Law is similar to English Law, but there are major differences.

have acquired some assets in the form of savings and property, get married or have dependants, you need to act responsibly and make a will, however simple, to clarify who gets what in the event of your decease. One lady I know made her first will at the ripe old age of 20!

THE ADVANTAGES OF TYING THE KNOT!

A friend of mine, a divorcee, had been living happily with another partner for several years, but neither of them had seen any point in tying the knot. However, when he looked into the possibility of buying a property in France he discovered to his chagrin that under French law his ex-wife and children would have a claim on his assets. (Scottish law is similar in this respect.) This prompted a rethink and he married his partner soon after.

In English law, too, unmarried couples, who may be treated as married partners in other respects, could encounter legal and financial problems when one partner dies. The surviving partner (unless officially designated next of kin) does not have any automatic right to a say in funeral arrangements and could miss out on various benefits or the partner's pension.

Another consideration is that if no will has been made any assets will automatically go to the deceased's blood relations, though it may be possible to mount a legal challenge. If there is a legal impediment to marrying, you could explore the idea of a Living Together Agreement – the Citizen's Advice Bureau or Advice Now website will have details – but this will not necessarily solve the problem. You have to make a will if you wish your partner to inherit.

Same sex partners who have registered their relationship under the Civil Partnership Act 2005 have a legal claim on the other's estate and may be eligible for other benefits, too, when one partner dies.

DRAWING UP A WILL

Basically a will sets out how your net assets (your estate) should be distributed, and nominates an executor (or executors) to carry out this task. To make the will valid your signature on it has to be witnessed by two people aged 18 or over, neither of whom or whose spouses will benefit from the will in any way, and who are together with you when the will is signed and dated.

This may seem such an easy process that you wonder why people bother with lawyers or professional will-makers. Certainly, DIY wills are perfectly admissable and you can buy special will forms from stationery shops and obtain will information packs from Age Concern and Help the Aged. However a handwritten or typed will on ordinary paper will serve the purpose just as well, provided it is signed and witnessed, since it is not the appearance of the document which is important, but the actual content (see Figure 2).

If your wishes are straighforward a DIY will may be perfectly adequate, but here I must sound a word of caution. Wills are legal documents and, as such, need to be carefully drafted. Careless wording can lead to unintended results and if the terms of the will are vague or unclear the will might have to go before a court for clarification.

For instance, 'I leave my estate to be divided among my family' may sound perfectly adequate to you, but it is a terribly vague sentence which could give rise to all kinds of

This is the Last Will and Testament of me Rodney George Orange of 25 White Horse Lane, Blackwater in the County of Surrey.

1. I hereby revoke all former wills.

2. I appoint my son Simon Arthur Orange of 7 Blue Vale Avenue, Blackwater and my daughter Lorna Geraldine Brown of 32 Greenhill Road, Blackwater to be the executors and trustees of this will.

3. I give and bequeath to each of my children Simon Arthur Orange and Lorna Geraldine Brown the sum of ten thousand pounds (£10,000). I give and bequeath to my grandson Edward Graham Brown the sum of five thousand pounds (£5,000) and to my nephew Richard Thomas Orange the sum of three thousand pounds (£3,000).

4. I give such car as I may own on my death and my porcelain collection to my sister Madeleine Audrey Orange.

5. I give my residuary estate to my wife Violet Edith Orange.

6. I wish my body to be buried.

7. My executors shall sell, call in and convert my property or such part as shall not consist of money with full power at their discretion to postpone such sale, calling in and conversion without being responsible for loss.

8. My executors shall pay or provide for out of such property and the proceeds of sale my funeral, testamentary and administration expenses and debts; all inheritance tax, estate duties and other imposts payable by reason of my death; and all legacies and annuities given by this will.

Dated 24 August 200X

Signed by the Testator (Testatrix) in our presence and then by us in the presence of the Testator (Testatrix)

Signature of Witness 1
(with name, address and occupation)

Signature of Witness 2
(with name, address and occupation)

Figure 2. Specimen will.

misunderstandings. By family do you mean your wife and children, or are all your sisters, brothers, cousins, uncles and aunts included? And do you mean to exclude anyone who is not a blood relation, such as a stepchild?

You also need to pose the question 'what if'? For example, what if one of your beneficiaries dies? Do you want his or her share to be redistributed among the other beneficiaries or should it go to the offspring of that person? And what if both you and your partner die together in a road accident? Who would inherit your estate then?

In order to avoid any confusion, you should write down the full name of each beneficiary (e.g. 'my sister Winifred Audrey Green or her children Teresa and Geoffrey Green if she should predecease me') and direct how you wish your assets to be apportioned among them. You could either state a lump sum or a percentage of your estate. The final beneficiary of your will receives what is left of your estate after the others have received their share. This is known as the residue.

You may include in your will instructions regarding your funeral and body or organ donation, but this could also be stated in an attached letter. Organ transplants can be a boon in prolonging the lives of others, and unfortunately demand exceeds supply. In addition to giving an indication in your will you should also inform the NHS Blood and Transplant agency and ideally carry a donor card on your person. There is also a demand for bodies for use in medical schools, and if you would like to donate your body for medical science, mention it in the will and inform a medical school or HM Inspector of Anatomy of your bequest.

It is customary to have a sentence in the document revoking any previous will you may have made, even though you may not have made one. This is just to indicate that this is definitely your last will and testament.

SHOULD A SOLICITOR DRAW UP THE WILL?

You do not have to use a solicitor, but a good case can be made for getting professional advice when drawing up your will to make sure that it is clear and reflects your true intentions. It is not expensive to engage the services of a solicitor or professional willwriter (think in terms of between £50 and £100 for a relatively straightforward will) and will offer you peace of mind.

The Law Society (of England and Wales, of Scotland or of Northern Ireland) can provide you with details of solicitors in your area, or you can look in *Yellow Pages*. The Institute of Professional Willmakers can supply you with a list of its members in your locality.

Before you visit your solicitor or will-maker, you ought to put down in writing what your assets are, how you wish them to be distributed and the full names of the beneficiaries. A good solicitor will be able to remove any ambiguities in the wording as well as recommend modifications to minimise liability to inheritance tax (currently 40 per cent once the threshold is exceeded). He can also deal with the creation of a trust for any beneficiaries who may not yet have reached their majority, to protect the family fortune, to ensure a beneficiary is looked after.

Generally speaking, the greater the value of your assets, the more you have to lose if the will is not precisely worded.

WHAT IS A MIRROR WILL?

These are near identical wills in which married partners leave everything to each other respectively and thereafter to their children or a named beneficiary if they have no offspring. A survivorship clause in the will should nominate an alternative beneficiary if the main beneficiary does not survive for a set period (usually 28 days) after the death. Where the partner is named as an executor it is important to nominate one extra executor in case both partners die at the same time.

UPDATING THE WILL

A will is not a document that is set in stone. It needs to reflect current rather than past realities and should therefore be revised periodically. After all, circumstances may change: some of your original beneficiaries may die; you may wish to leave a bequest to new arrivals such as a child or grandchild; you may acquire additional property not mentioned in the previous will; you may get married or divorced; or one of your executors may have died or become incapable of discharging their function.

Minor changes can be incorporated into the will by inserting additional paragraphs, known as codicils, which have to be witnessed. However, it is preferable to draw up a new will as you would certainly need to do if there were a major change in your circumstances, such as marriage or divorce. Even if no drastic changes occur in you life, it does no harm to revisit your will at regular intervals – say, every five or ten years – to make sure that it continues to reflect your wishes.

PREPARE FOR THE UNEXPECTED

The importance of keeping a will up-to-date was demonstrated when a great-aunt of mine died. Her widowed husband arranged for the solicitor to call on him the following week so that he could alter the provisions of the will he had made some decades earlier. Alas, he died hours before the solicitor arrived, and so the estate was distributed according to the rules of intestacy to distant relations whom he scarcely knew rather than the people he would have wanted to be his heirs.

Once you have made the will it is advisable to give copies of it to your executors (and perhaps also to your next of kin) and store the original in a safe place where it can be easily found. If you have employed a solicitor they will doubtless offer to keep it in their office vaults; alternatively it could be lodged with your bank, the National Will Register or the Will Registry Office.

ONE WILL OR TWO?

Normally the only will which has legal authority is the one you made most recently. However, if you have assets outside the UK – a holiday home on the Algarve, for instance – it could be advantageous to make a second will in the country concerned. By doing this you will speed up the legal procedures involved in disposing of your foreign assets.

You should get advice from a solicitor either in the country concerned or employ a UK-based solicitor who is licensed to practise the law of the country concerned. A list of these can be found in *How to Retire Abroad.*

LISTING YOUR ASSETS AND LIABILITIES

A problem that some executors are confronted with when they come to administer the estate of a dead person is that details of the deceased's assets and the relevant documentation are hidden away. This can be a particular difficulty in the case of people who have been living on their own and have not confided in anyone.

Unfortunately, the executors cannot get the authority to prove the will until they have submitted the *Return of Estate Information Form* to HM Customs and Revenue, which itemises the liabilities and assets of the estate. For this reason you need to list any property you own, any outstanding loans or mortgages you have taken out, and provide details of your bank and building society accounts, insurance policies, investments, National Savings and Premium Bonds, etc. It is not necessary to provide a valuation, as the value of many investments is subject to fluctuation.

Once you have made your list, you can either give copies to your executors and next of kin or place it in a sealed envelope with words to the effect that it is to be opened only after your death. It should be lodged securely with your solicitor, bank or the Will Registry Office and copies given to your designated executors.

See Figure 3 for an example of the things you should include in your list.

INHERITANCE TAX

The rise in property prices in recent years has meant that an increasing number of estates attract inheritance tax (IHT) of 40 per cent. Nobody wants to pay tax at this rate if they can possibly avoid it, so it would be prudent to assess whether the value of your estate is likely to be above the current IHT threshold (£285,000 in 2006/7, £300,000 in 2007/8 and £312,000 in 2008/9) and, if so, take action to reduce liability, by giving away some of your assets while you are alive, for instance.

There are, however, restrictions on the amount you can give away. The annual limit for large gifts is £3,000, but you can make as many gifts of up to £250 as you wish. You can also make wedding gifts of up to £5,000 to each child, up to £2,500 to each grandchild and up to £1,000 to others.

Assets and liabilities of John Gresham born 1931

Property: 23 Sparrow Row, Finchtown.
(deeds with Bird & Co solicitors, Finchtown)

Bank: Peacock's Bank, Lark Place Branch, Finchtown: Current Account Number: 98765432 (Cheque book in top drawer of writing desk.)

Building society: Mortgage with Crane Building Society, Chaffinch Street Branch, Finchtown: Reference TTTMBFT. (Documentation in top drawer of writing desk.)

Insurance: House insurance with Albatross Insurance: Policy No: 76543219 arranged by Nightingale Insurance Brokers, Lark Place, Finchtown. (Policy in top drawer of writing desk.)

Life insurance: Woodpecker Assurance Ltd: Policy No: ZY234789 arranged by Nightingale Insurance Brokers. (In writing desk.)

Miscellaneous investments: Managed by Eagle Investments, Squirrel Terrace, Finchtown.

Private Pension Plan: Curlew Pensions Ltd, Curlew House, Magpie Row, Finchtown: Reference: 5559988.

National Savings: Premium Bond Certificates worth £2,500: Holder No 676898121.

Funeral plan: Swallow Funeral Plan with Nightingale Insurance Brokers.

Electricity supplier: Raven Utilities, 19–23 Barn Owl Way, Swallow Wells. A/C 1234567. (Recent bills in writing desk.)

Water supplier: Swift Water Co, 14 Cormorant Street, Kingfisher Springs. (Recent bills in writing desk.)

Telephone provider: Robin Telecom, 20 Lapwing Avenue, Dovetown. A/C 9876543. (Recent bills in writing desk.)

Figure 3. Specimen list of assets and liabilities.

Fortunately, there are exemptions – parts of your estate which do not attract inheritance tax. Where spouses own a property jointly or operate a joint bank account the transfer of assets to the surviving joint owner is normally exempt from IHT. Bequests to registered charities, business assets, agricultural property, woodland and National Heritage property are also exempt. It may be possible to mitigate some tax liability by creating a trust, but it is essential to obtain professional advice from a solicitor or an accountant if you intend to do so.

The good news is that currently 94 per cent of estates do not attract inheritance tax. One reason for this could be that many far-sighted individuals take steps to limit liability to this tax before they die.

PLANNING YOUR FUNERAL

Some wills specify the kind of funeral the deceased would like to have, though more often than not this is left to the discretion of those who survive you. However, there is no reason why you should not indicate your preferences to your next of kin. Brief details can be incorporated in your will or set down in writing.

ONE FINAL TASK

An acquaintance of mine lay in a hospital bed in the final stages of a terminal illness. This was clearly a depressing time for him, but he used his final days to good advantage by mapping out in some detail the form of funeral service he would like – including the readings, hymns and prayers. His family were only too happy to carry out his wishes knowing that they were honouring his memory in the way he wished.

Here are some points to consider:

◆ Burial or cremation: cremation is becoming the more popular method, but adherents of certain religions (e.g. Islam, orthodox Judaism) will normally specify burial.

◆ The form of ceremony: most funerals will conform to the practices of the major religions – Anglican, Catholic, Quaker, Buddhist, etc. However, if you are not a believer it is possible to have a secular funeral with no reference to an afterlife. While you could dispense with a funeral altogether, bear in mind that a funeral ceremony is for the benefit of the bereaved as well as yourself and a good funeral – as opposed to a very minimal affair – will assist them in their grieving.

◆ The place of the funeral: many funerals are held at a cemetery or crematorium chapel, but if you have links with a particular place of worship you may prefer to have it there. Some funerals are quiet family affairs and are followed later by a more public service of thanksgiving for the life of the deceased.

◆ The place of burial: for instance, you can indicate if there is a family grave or vault where you wish to be buried, or you may choose to have your ashes scattered in a particular spot. There is a trend these days to be buried in nature reserves or woodland, the addresses of which are listed in *The Natural Death Handbook*.

◆ The funeral officiant: you may have a particular person in mind whom you would like to conduct the funeral – your local parish priest or a family friend, for instance. It is sensible to suggest alternatives, just in case the person in question is unavailable.

◆ Music (and hymns, in the case of the Christian funeral)
which you would like during the service: is there any music
for which you have a particular affection?

◆ Flowers or donations: it is increasingly common to ask
mourners to make a donation to a nominated charity (such
as the British Heart Foundation) in lieu of sending flowers.

◆ Hospitality after the funeral: why not give your assent to a
reception afterwards to restore people's spirits after the
serious business of the funeral service?

When considering the form of your funeral you might also
consider which funeral director you would like to use (if
indeed you wish to use one at all) and pass on your
recommendations to your next of kin. After a person's death
the next of kin are under pressure to appoint a funeral director
as quickly as possible and rarely have time to shop around.

At funeral and memorial services it is customary to include a
short account of the deceased's life, unless you expressly
forbid it. Sometimes precise information is hard to come by at
short notice, particularly if you have outlived most of your
contemporaries and the funeral organisers do not have time
on their side to search for it. So it would be a worthwhile
exercise to set down the main points of your life (with dates)
in writing for the person paying the tribute to refer to. For an
example of how this could be done see Figure 4.

Biographical Details of Phoebe Rose Seymour

Born Phoebe Rose Fletcher on 6 May 1925 in Birmingham.

Parents: Gordon Samuel and Dorothy Lily Fletcher.

Brothers and sisters: Frank and Georgina.

Family moved to Grove Park, Rosewood in 1930.

Attended St Martin's Primary School, Rosewood 1930–1936 and then Rosewood Grammar School for Girls 1936–1942. Played hockey for the First XI and took part in school plays.

Trained as a nurse at Hollybush Royal Infirmary 1942–1945.

In 1944 her father was killed in action in Northern France.

Worked at Firtrees Hospital, Bristol from 1945 to 1950.

Met future husband Oliver Jack Seymour at a hospital dance in 1949.

Married Oliver on March 30th 1950 at St Silas' Church, Birch Green, Somerset.

Moved with Oliver to Appletree, Lincolnshire in 1951; worked part-time at Lincoln General Hospital and Oliver worked as a civil servant.

Became a full-time housewife when son Gerald was born in 1952. A second child, Deborah, was born in 1954.

In 1969 resumed nursing career at the Willows Nursing Home in Appletree.

Led an active social life as a member of the Appletree Women's Institute and the local Choral Society.

On retirement in 1975 did charity work for the local hospice and Help the Aged.

Also studied for an Open University degree in Biology.

In 1983 when Oliver died of lung cancer, moved to Bushley, Norfolk to be closer to daughter Deborah.

Became an active member of the Bushley Readers' Circle and did volunteer work for Bushley Museum and Victim Support.

Moved in with daughter and son-in-law in 2000 due to failing health.

Dated 30 September 2002

Figure 4. Sample biographical summary.

FINANCING THE FUNERAL

The costs of a funeral are normally paid for out of your estate, but there can be a delay before these funds become available. This is not always a problem, as your bank or building society may be prepared to advance money to pay for the funeral before probate is granted, or the funeral directors may delay the demand for payment if asked to.

One way to circumvent such a problem is to pay into a funeral plan which will release the cash when the funeral director submits the invoice. There are a number of firms on the market, such as Golden Charter, Golden Leaves, schemes administered by Age Concern and Help the Aged and some run by funeral directors themselves.

As a precaution you should only take out a plan affiliated to either the National Association for Pre-paid Funeral Plans (NAPFP) or the Funeral Planning Council and approved by the Funeral Planning Authority. Prices usually start at around £1,500 and are payable either in instalments or in a lump sum. However, it is important to read the small print very carefully to see if your payment is guaranteed to cover the full cost of the funeral or if extra charges will be payable if the plan is not fully paid up. Some of the more popular plans are to be found in the *Useful Addresses* section of this book.

Some trade unions and other mutual associations pay out funeral benefits to their members. You might also consider taking out a life assurance policy or opening a deposit account for the express purpose of paying your funeral expenses.

It is important to advise your next of kin or executor of any financial arrangements you may have made, and particularly if you have paid into a funeral plan as this may restrict the choice of funeral director.

Chapters 3 and 4 deal with funeral arrangements in detail.

AS THE END DRAWS CLOSER

Some elderly people remain in reasonable health and in full possession of their faculties right up until the day they die. Others, particularly if they attain a great age or suffer from a debilitating terminal illness, become increasingly frail and dependent on others – a stage which could last days, weeks or years. Rather than assume that this could never happen to you, you should plan for such an eventuality.

Living independently

Most older people would prefer to live out their days in their own home, rather than go into residential accommodation and lose their independence. If you are of this mind, you should investigate what forms of assistance are available to you – both statutory and voluntary.

The local branch of Age Concern or Help the Aged will be able to provide you with details of local facilities, such as meals on wheels, day centres and home care assistance. You may well be eligible for financial help in the form of an attendance allowance, which would help offset the cost of home care and hospital transport. Many doctors' surgeries have community nurses attached to them who can assess your needs and obtain the assistance you need.

If you have difficulty in getting about you could apply for a disabled parking permit from the local council, enabling you (or whoever is driving you) to park in restricted areas. Financial help may also be forthcoming to install chairlifts and railings in your home.

Don't be afraid to ask around about the facilities that are open to you. Anything which makes the evening of your life comfortable and more bearable is well worth exploring.

Living with others
The time may come when you are no longer able to cope, and you may consider moving in with a member of your family, typically a son or daughter. But such arrangements do not always work out satisfactorily and you should endeavour to have a trial run first of all.

Where you are being cared for by a relation or friend, you ought to ensure that they are being offered sufficient help both from the state and the voluntary sectors. I have already mentioned such matters as the attendance allowance and day centres; the organisation Carers UK can provide you with details as to what services and benefits are available to take some of the pressure off those who are looking after you.

Another consideration is that living with your children could well involve moving to another part of the country with which you are unfamiliar, whereas you would prefer to remain in a locality where you have plenty of friends and acquaintances. In this case it makes sense to explore other options, preferably while you are still active.

Sheltered housing offers a certain degree of independence, and you have the reassurance that there is someone keeping an eye on you. A retirement home provides you with all your daily needs – meals, cleaning, etc – and, not least, companionship. If your condition is very grave you will need to find a comfortable nursing home or hospice offering palliative care. Consult with your next of kin to reach the best solution.

Enduring power of attorney
If you are elderly, when you come to make your will the solicitor may suggest that you make an enduring power of attorney agreement. This is a sensible precaution just in case one day you are no longer able to manage your affairs. It enables someone else to sign cheques, enter into agreements for you and carry out other transactions on your behalf. Information on the process is available from the Public Guardianship Office. It is sensible to appoint two attorneys in case one of them dies.

The enduring power of attorney need not take effect immediately. You simply make an agreement which can be activated at some time in the future by the person or persons you have nominated to act on your behalf. In order to do so, a form has to be obtained from the Public Guardianship Office or downloaded from its website. The person designated as your attorney has to give notice of their intention to do so to you and your next of kin, who have the right to lodge objections. There are a number of safeguards, and at any time the agreement can be revoked.

Medical power of attorney and living wills
If you have a serious terminal medical condition, and do not wish your life to be prolonged unnecessarily, you might consider making a medical power of attorney which enables a designated person to make medical decisions on your behalf if you should become unable to make or communicate such decisions yourself.

A living will fulfils a similar function by setting out your wishes in writing regarding medical treatment and intervention. The legal status of such wills is unclear, but doctors and other healthcare staff would doubtless respect any directions you may have made. They are often faced with difficult decisions, such as whether to resuscitate a person if the chances of survival are slim, or whether to relieve pain with drugs which could have the effect of shortening a person's life. They would doubtless welcome clear directions from you or your next of kin as to your true wishes.

If you are considering going down either of these avenues, you should discuss the matter with your next of kin and medical staff and obtain their agreement, since this is not a decision to be taken lightly. The instructions can be revoked at any time.

The Natural Death Association and the Voluntary Euthanasia Society can provide information about living wills, as well as guidelines on making one.

Spiritual and emotional comfort

I am aware that I have devoted most of this chapter to practical matters and have tended to ignore emotional needs. It would be most unfortunate if those around you are so taken up with attending to your physical requirements that they have no time to spend with you. As a person's life draws to a close, visitors can be a great source of comfort, even if they stay for only a brief period of time.

Some people may be put off visiting you because they do not wish to disturb you, but you should indicate that everyone is most welcome, even if you cannot offer them scintillating conversation. In time they might come to regret that they did not pay a final visit to you while you were still alive.

If you have been a regular attender at a local church or synagogue in the past your local parish priest or rabbi will probably come to see you as a matter of course, but if the congregation is a large one, a request may have to be given.

If you are not attached to a particular religious grouping, you need not miss out on clerical visits. A message to the appropriate authorities should suffice. In hospitals there are usually chaplains on hand to offer reassurance and cater for your spiritual needs.

It is not unusual for people on their deathbeds to seek spiritual comfort and most clergymen are adept at putting the sick and dying at their ease. They will pray with you and administer holy communion or last rites – depending on your religious persuasion.

Unfinished business

Are there any family problems or misunderstandings that need to be sorted out before you pass on? It is not unknown for friends or family members to fall out and in your final days you are in a strong position to effect a reconciliation.

Also, there may be people who have been particularly kind and considerate to you whom you need to thank personally, and those who will miss you badly who would benefit from words of reassurance from you. Don't put it off until you are no longer capable of speech.

I have already stressed the importance of tidying up your affairs before the end, and this includes your financial affairs. If you sense your days are limited it would be sensible to call in your next of kin and executors to clarify any instructions you have made and ensure they know how to access the relevant documentation. The checklist in Figure 5 could serve as a model.

Information for My Next of Kin and Executors

Name
Address
Date of birth
Place of birth
NI number
NHS card number
Passport number
Dependants
Doctor
Employer
Solicitor
Accountant
Bank
Building society
Pension/benefit details
Landlord
Tenant(s)
Other people to be informed of my death
Funeral instructions

Location of
   Birth certificate
   Credit and debit cards
   Driving licence
   Funeral plan
   Income tax documents
   Insurance policies
   Keys to property/properties
   Loan agreements
   Marriage certificate
   Mortgage agreement
   Will
   Medical card
   Organ donation consent
   Passport
   Saving books
   Share certificates
   National Savings and Premium Bond certificates
   Rental agreements
   Vehicle registration document
(Any items which do not apply should be deleted.)

Figure 5. Checklist for next of kin and executors.

2

When Death Occurs

The death of someone you know, even if it has been anticipated, can come as a shock; if it is unexpected it can be a body blow. However the next of kin may have little time to fret and grieve at first, for the next few days will involve a period of intense activity, when a clear head is needed for several important decisions.

First things first. In the immediate aftermath of the death there are a number of tasks which have priority over all others. They are:

- reporting the death

- making arrangements for the care of the body

- obtaining certification of the death

- registering the death

- notifying relatives, friends and interested parties.

REPORTING A DEATH

Death in a hospital or other institution

If the death occurs in hospital (or a hospice, nursing home or retirement home), well rehearsed procedures are in place to deal with the situation. Normally medical staff can tell intuitively if a person's last hours have come and they will inform the next of kin so that they can pay a final visit.

After death a medical certificate is issued by the doctor in charge of the patient and this will normally need to be collected by the next of kin.

Death at home

In England and Wales one in every five deaths occurs at home. (In Scotland and other countries the proportion is around 30 per cent.)

If you are the first to discover the body, you may feel confused and distraught, but you must try to suppress such feelings in order to carry out some important tasks.

You will need first to get a doctor – the patient's GP (if known) – to confirm that the person is dead and arrange for the issuance of a medical certificate giving the cause of death.

More often than not the first person to be aware of the death will be the deceased's next of kin (such as a spouse, parent or child) or at least a close friend of the deceased. If not, the person finding the body will need to get in touch with all due speed with the deceased's nearest relative or whoever is entrusted with handling the deceased's affairs, since these are the people empowered to make decisions relating to the deceased. If they live at a distance, they may be happy to delegate authority.

DEATH IN THE NIGHT

My mother died at home in the middle of the night when her doctor was off duty. I phoned the doctor's surgery and the answerphone directed me to the out of hours medical service. It was a doctor from this service who came to examine her and confirm that she was dead. Then he gave permission for the body to be taken away and promised to email her own doctor who would issue the medical certificate and be in touch with me.

However, the message had obviously gone astray as I heard nothing, so I had to ring up the surgery in the morning. After that matters went smoothly and I was able to collect the medical certificate the following day.

None of her close relations expressed a wish to see her body, since they had seen her recently when she was still alive, so arrangements were made with a representative of a firm of funeral directors who came to remove the body during the course of the morning.

Death away from home

In a minority of cases death occurs away from home – while on holiday, for instance. When this happens, you – or the person who finds the body – will need to seek out a medical practitioner who can confirm that the person is dead. Also, if you are not the next of kin, you need to inform whoever is of what has happened without delay.

If the death has occurred abroad, you should find out about local procedures for reporting the death, as these may differ from those in England and Wales. If you need advice on how to proceed, you should contact the local police or the nearest British consulate where you will need to register the death of a British national. Registration can also be done through the Overseas Section of the General Register Office (or the equivalent office in Scotland or Northern Ireland).

If the person has travel insurance the company should be contacted to see if the policy has any provision for the recovery of the costs of repatriating the body.

MOVING THE BODY

If the death occurred in hospital, the body is usually despatched to the hospital mortuary for collection after a medical certificate has been issued. Nursing homes and hospices will ask the next of kin to make arrangements for the body to be taken away or arrange for a funeral director to do this.

Where a death occurs at home the doctor who examines the body and confirms the death will let you know if the body can be moved. If the death was unexpected, the body may have to go to hospital for a post mortem.

In the past it was customary in some families to keep the body at home – typically in the front parlour – until the day of the funeral so that relatives and friends could come to pay their respects. This tradition has now gone out of fashion, but it would be wise to check whether any close relative wishes to view the deceased at home before the body is taken away.

Nowadays most people prefer to employ funeral directors (undertakers) to take the body to their premises and keep it there until the day of the funeral. After the funeral director has taken charge of the body there will be an opportunity to see the deceased again, lying in a coffin in the funeral director's chapel of rest, but prior arrangement is needed.

Since the body will normally be ready for removal within hours of a person's death, you will need to contact a funeral director with all due speed. Ideally you will have a firm in mind, but if the death was unexpected you may not have thought about such matters. Chapter 3 offers advice on using funeral directors.

OBTAINING A MEDICAL CERTIFICATE

Deaths seem to involve a considerable amount of red tape which newly bereaved people may find bewildering and infuriating. A seemingly endless number of organisations have to be contacted, but you will normally find that the people you deal with are sympathetic and helpful.

It is important to prioritise your actions. The first thing that needs to be done in the hours following a death is to obtain a medical certificate – or at least set in motion the mechanism to get one. Without one of these the death cannot be registered, and without the death certificate the funeral cannot take place.

Normally the doctor who has been treating the deceased will issue a medical certificate indicating the cause of death. This is not for your eyes, but will be in a sealed envelope and addressed to the Registrar of Births, Marriages and Deaths in the local area. The doctor will also often issue a formal notice (*Notice to Informant*) saying that the medical certificate has been signed and giving instructions on how to register the death, which should normally be carried out within five days of the decease (or eight days in the case of Scotland).

If the death occurred suddenly or unexpectedly, matters may not be so straightforward. The doctor or doctors treating the patient may wish to investigate the cause of death, and will ask permission of the relatives to carry out a post-mortem examination. This is not something you need worry about and should not be taken as an indication that they suspect foul play.

In certain circumstances, notably an accident or injury, a sudden and unexplained death, or a death during an operation or under anaesthetic, it may be decided to report the death to the coroner (or procurator fiscal in Scotland). A report to the coroner is also necessary if the doctor treating the deceased had not seen him or her after death or during the 14 days before death.

Such a decision may well delay the issue of the medical certificate and so other arrangements, such as the funeral, may have to be postponed. If the coroner decides a post-mortem examination of the body or an inquest is needed, some considerable time could elapse before the body can be released. The death cannot be registered without the coroner's permission.

BURIAL OR CREMATION?

One decision that has to be made very soon after the death is whether the body is to be buried or cremated. Cremation is by far the most popular method in the UK – over 70 per cent of people dying in the UK are cremated. It is normally a far cheaper option since you do not have the expense of a gravestone or burial plot, which can be particularly expensive in urban areas where land for burial is scarce.

However, you need to take into account the deceased's wishes and the practices of the deceased's religion. Muslims and most Jews, for instance, traditionally opt for burial. The Cremation Society of Great Britain can explain what is involved and offer advice.

If you decide on cremation, you should inform the doctor who makes out the medical certificate and he will sign an additional certificate authorising cremation. It is a legal requirement that two certificates (B and C) – or rather two sections of the same certificate – are signed by different doctors. You will receive a telephone call from a second doctor who is independent of the first one and who will ask you brief questions relating to the circumstances of the deceased's death. This is very much a formality and it should not cause you any concern.

One of the doctors will ask for the name of the funeral director and forward the certificates to this address. If you are doing all the funeral arrangements yourself, they should be sent direct to the crematorium or burial authorities.

REGISTERING A DEATH

Once the medical certificate stating the cause of death from the doctor or hospital is available, it has to be taken to a Registrar of Births, Marriages and Deaths who will register the death and issue a death certificate. Normally this is done in the locality (sub-district) where the death occurred, but if this proves a problem any registrar can handle this procedure.

The person who registers the death is known as an informant, and in normal circumstances is either a relative present at the time of death or during the final illness, a relative who lives in the same district as the deceased, a person present at the death or who found the body, the occupier of the building where the death occurred, or the person responsible for the funeral.

If the doctor or hospital does not tell you where you have to register the death, the address can be found in the appropriate telephone directory under Registration of Births, Marriages and Deaths or on the website www.gro.gov.uk (www.

gro-scotland.gov.uk in Scotland and www.groni.gov.uk in Northern Ireland). Alternatively you can ask at the local council offices, post office or police station.

As mentioned earlier the death must be registered within five days of its occurrence (eight days in Scotland) unless the Registrar gives permission to exceed this limit. If a coroner is involved, however, registration cannot take place until the registrar has received authority from the coroner.

Making an appointment

The registration entails a personal visit to the Registry Office and since some registry offices have restricted opening hours it makes sense to telephone beforehand to make an appointment. Some operate an appointments system as a matter of course, and if you turn up on spec you may have a long wait.

In addition to the medical certificate stating the cause of death you should take along

◆ the deceased's medical card, if available

◆ the deceased's birth certificate, if available

◆ the deceased's marriage certificate, if applicable and available.

You should also be prepared to answer questions about the deceased of the following nature:

- the date and place of death

- the deceased's last address

- the deceased's full name – first name(s), surname and maiden name (if applicable)

- the deceased's date and place of birth

- the deceased's occupation

- the name and occupation of the deceased's spouse (if applicable)

- whether the deceased was getting a pension or allowance from public funds

- the date of birth of the surviving widow/widower of the deceased (if applicable).

In Scotland you will also be required to provide the exact time of death, together with details of the deceased's mother and father and whether they are still alive.

The whole registration procedure takes between 20 and 30 minutes.

GETTING THE NAMES RIGHT

Accuracy is important, not least with regard to the name of the deceased in order to avoid confusion in the future. Some people may alter the spelling of their name or change their names completely during the course of their lives.

In the case of my mother the forenames on her birth certificate differed slightly from those on her marriage and death certificates. She had changed the spelling of her first name and suppressed the second forename because she did not like it. In the interests of correctness the Registrar entered both the names by which she had been known on the registration certificate.

Issue of documentation

After you have provided the Registrar with the necessary details, they will enter the details into the death register (which you have to sign) and issue you with one certified copy of the entry – known as the Death Certificate (see Figure 6). Further embossed copies are available on payment of a fee.

Is there any point in getting further copies? In most cases yes, because a number of organisations – such as the deceased's bank, pension fund managers, insurance companies, etc – may well wish to have evidence of the death before they can release funds. Professional advisers – such as solicitors and accountants – will also wish to see the Death Certificate before they can act. Photocopies are not usually acceptable.

Fortunately, most organisations will not want to keep the certified copy, but will normally return it to you once they

---

CERTIFIED COPY OF AN ENTRY
DEATH

Registration District:

Administrative area:

Sub-district:

1. Date and place of death:

2. Name and surname:

3. Sex:

4. Maiden surname of woman who has married:

5. Date and place of birth:

6. Occupation and usual address:

7a. Name and surname of informant:

7b. Qualification of informant:

7c. Usual address of informant:

8. Cause of death:
    Certified by (name of doctor)

9. I certify that the particulars given by me above are true to the best of my
    knowledge and belief
    (Signature of Informant)

10. Date of Registration

11. Signature of registrar

Figure 6. Death Certificate details.

have seen it. So it is not strictly speaking necessary to get certificates to send to each one.

Although registering the death costs nothing, additional copies of the death certificate cost £3.50 in 2005, a sum which increases to £7 after one month. In my mother's case I asked for five copies, and that proved to be sufficient. Although nearly double that number of organisations wanted proof of her death, they all returned the documents after seeing them.

The Registrar will also issue you with a Certificate of Registration of Death (BD8) which needs to be completed and taken or sent to the local social security office or Job Centre of the Department for Work and Pensions.

You will also be given what is known as the Green Form – the *Certificate for Burial or Cremation* which has to be given to the funeral director – or the crematorium, cemetery or burial ground authorities if this is to be a DIY funeral. (In Northern Ireland the form is actually white, while in Scotland there is no Green Form to show to the funeral director as a certificate of registration of death will suffice.)

If the body is to be taken out of England and Wales you need to obtain Form 103 from the coroner. In Scotland no special documentation is needed. You should enquire at the consulate of the destination country what documentation is needed with the body.

Incidentally the Registrar may be able to provide you with a useful free booklet entitled *What to Do After a Death in England and Wales* (D49), describing the procedures you need to go through. Scotland and Northern Ireland have similar literature.

DONATING A BODY OR ORGANS

Some bereaved people are too upset when a person has just died to want to discuss donating the body for medical research or organ transplants. Indeed they may well take umbrage if the subject is mooted.

Personally, I would be delighted if parts of my body could be used to alleviate suffering or prolong the life of someone else after I am gone. With this end in view I carry an organ donor card and am registered with the Organ Donor Register of the NHS Blood and Transplant agency.

If the deceased has expressed a wish to donate their organs or body, the usual procedure is for the hospital to approach the next of kin to ensure they have no objections. Unfortunately, decisions have to be made in what you may regard as indecent haste, before the organs start to deteriorate, and signatures will be required giving consent. In the case of organ removal the body will be returned to the next of kin for burial after the organs have been removed. Normally organs are not taken for transplants if the donor is over 75.

If the body is to be used for medical research, the medical school in question may keep a whole body for teaching purposes for up to three years. After this time they will arrange and pay for a simple burial or release the body to the relatives. However, if the body is unsuitable, the authorities may turn down the offer.

NOTIFYING RELATIONS AND FRIENDS

One of the most harrowing tasks the next of kin has to face up to is notifying friends and relations of the death.

In the past it was customary to send notification of a death by post, often in black-edged envelopes, but in these days of rapid communication it is more usual to phone people or communicate with them by email.

If there is a long list of people to be notified, be prepared to delegate the task (or some of it) to others. In many cases they will be only too willing to be of service at this difficult time. Ideally you should make a list of the people you need to inform and tick them off as you contact them.

How do you find out who you need to notify and how to get in touch with them? It is perhaps too much to hope for that the deceased will have a list of contacts to be notified, as recommended in Chapter 1. But most people possess address books and it is worth hunting round for these. My mother had no fewer than three, not all of which were up to date.

When telephoning try to keep your message short and simple. You may find it helpful to write down what you intend to say. Prepare people for the worst by starting off with words such as 'I'm afraid I have some bad news', and then 'my father Fred Alder has just died'. I recommend including the name with the relationship – your aunt Hermione Brown, your cousin Harry Greenwood – and using the verb 'die' rather than euphemisms such as 'passed away' or 'passed on' in the interests of clarity. Some of the people you contact will be elderly and suffer from hearing problems, and if you have bad news to impart, you don't want to have to repeat it.

The recipients of the call will doubtless express sympathy and shock, and may well ask for brief details of how and when the person died. Some will ask about the funeral arrangements, but as this information is unlikely to be known at this stage, you should offer to notify them at a future date. Make a note of this so that you do not forget them.

If you do not have a telephone number for certain people you feel should be contacted, send a brief note by first class mail and include your telephone number or email address (see Figure 7). You may wish to use special cards or notelets

---

38 Ash Lane
Pinedale
Surrey
PP5 8VS
11 April 200X

Dear Beatrice,

I am sorry to inform you that my sister Clothilde Wood passed away yesterday, 10th April, at Alderham General Hospital after a short illness. We shall all remember her with great affection.

   The funeral arrangements have yet to be finalised, but if you wish, I will let you have the details in due course.

Regards
George (Maple)
Tel: 01234 567890
Email: gmaple@britnet.co.uk.

Figure 7. Letter announcing a death.

available from stationers, but ordinary notepaper is quite acceptable.

Until you have details of the funeral it is best to delay placing a death announcement in the press. However, if the deceased was a prominent member of the community you may wish to inform the news editor of the local newspaper or news agency of the death. This matter is dealt with at greater length in the next chapter.

3

Engaging a Funeral Director

Funeral directors (or undertakers, as they used to be known) are responsible for much more than just arranging funerals. They take the body away to their premises, keep it until the funeral, place it in a coffin, make the arrangements for burial or cremation and, finally, deliver the deceased to the cemetery, churchyard or crematorium. In certain circumstances they may embalm the body.

Appointing a funeral director normally has to be done fairly quickly once a death has occurred, particularly if the death occurred in a hospice or nursing home where there are no facilities for keeping a corpse. If the death occurred in hospital there will be less urgency about removing the body as it is usually placed in the mortuary to await collection.

PLANNING AHEAD
In an ideal world funeral arrangements would be planned in advance while the person is still alive. However we sometimes find ourselves overtaken by events – such as an unexpected death – where arrangements have to be made in what may seem inordinate haste where you have little, if any, time to shop around and compare prices and services.

Fortunately, not everything has to be decided right from the start and if you prioritise what has to be done the task will seem much more manageable.

The first step is to arrange for the body to be taken away and cared for until the funeral.

Once you have obtained the death certificate you can then give the funeral director the go-ahead to fix a date, time and place for the funeral. Most funerals I have attended have taken place within a week or so of the death.

If there has to be a post-mortem there will be some delay in the issue of a death certificate, and the funeral date may have to be put back.

The final details of the funeral can be left for a further day or two, so you will be able to consult with close relations and friends of the deceased as to what form the service should take.

CHOOSING A FUNERAL DIRECTOR

While it is perfectly feasible to take responsibility for all of the funeral arrangements yourself, normally only the most committed and enterprising of us do so. At the end of this chapter we recount the experiences of someone with experience of arranging a DIY funeral.

Most people prefer to entrust the funeral arrangements to a funeral director. This takes some of the burden off your shoulders at a busy time and should ensure that the whole procedure goes off smoothly.

Sometimes the choice of funeral director has already been made for you. For instance, the deceased may have left instructions as to which firm should be used, or may have paid into a funeral plan whose administrators may specify which firms you are able to use. However, those in charge of the funeral are entitled to exercise their discretion in this matter.

In most cases funeral directors tend to be chosen on the strength of their reputation rather than the competitiveness of their fees, and it makes sense to ask around for recommendations. Doctors and clergymen will know of the main firms in their area, and *The Natural Death Handbook* makes its own recommendations. *Yellow Pages* will list all the funeral directors within a given area.

You could also approach the two trade associations for details of firms in the locality. These are the National Association of Funeral Directors (the larger of the two with over 3,000 members) and the National Society of Allied and Independent Funeral Directors. Some firms belong to both. Both the NAFD and SAIF have a strict code of practice which their members agree to observe, which is a good reason for choosing one of them. If the firm employs staff with a professional qualification in funeral management, so much the better.

The majority of funeral directors are small independent firms. Some have been taken over by larger companies, such as Dignity, although they may retain their original name. The leading provider of funeral services in the UK is the Co-op, which arranges around 25 per cent of all funerals in the UK.

If the deceased died in a hospice or nursing home, the manager may have an arrangement with a particular funeral director to take the body away, particularly if there is some delay in contacting the next of kin. You have the option of continuing to use this particular firm or appointing another firm.

Non-Christian religious groups have special requirements as to how funerals are arranged, and you should make sure that the firm you employ is aware of these. The local mosque, temple or synagogue will be able to advise you and may point you in the direction of funeral directors which specialise in arranging such funerals, such as the Asian Funeral Service in North London.

WHO PAYS FOR THE FUNERAL?

The person arranging the funeral is ultimately responsible for ensuring that the bill is paid. Normally the costs will be borne by the estate of the deceased, so it is important to check with the executors of the will that sufficient funds are available before going ahead. You should also investigate whether provision has been made for funeral payments from:

+ a prepaid funeral plan

+ a life assurance policy

+ a pension scheme offering help with funeral costs

+ death benefits from a friendly society or trade union.

A Funeral Payment from the Department of Work and Pensions' Social Fund may be payable if the deceased appears to have inadequate funds to pay for the funeral. However, the payment may not cover the full cost of a basic funeral and the DWP has the right to reclaim some of the cost from the deceased's estate or close relatives, except in the case of war pensioners. Application for the payment must be made to the local social security office on Form SF200 within three months of the funeral.

You can get further information on entitlements from such organisations as the Citizens' Advice Bureau and Cruse Bereavement Care.

In cases where the deceased has no next of kin, the local council or the hospital where the person died takes responsibility for the funeral and normally appoints the funeral director. Both have the right to recoup some or all of the costs from the estate.

Bear in mind that there could be some delay in obtaining funds from the deceased's estate or from other sources, though the deceased's bank or building society will often be willing to release funds to cover the funeral expenses. If you envisage any problems in settling the bill on time you should inform the funeral directors accordingly. Most will be sympathetic and agree for payments to be deferred or paid in instalments, but such arrangements may incur interest. Most firms nowadays accept payment by credit card.

WHAT COSTS ARE INVOLVED?

Most people adopt the view that they wish to give the deceased a good send-off regardless of cost, but some react differently when they receive the funeral director's invoice. As this book went to press funeral bills in excess of £2,000 were quite normal and I attended one which cost twice that figure.

Jessica Mitford's book *The American Way of Death Revisited* describes the astronomical prices being charged for some funerals on the other side of the Atlantic. Prices in the UK are fairly modest in comparison; even so the cost of dying is not getting any cheaper.

A survey of 100 funeral directors by the insurance company American Life published at the beginning of 2006 revealed that over the past six years funeral costs had increased by 61 per cent. The average burial will now set you back £3,307 and the average cremation £1,954, but there is considerable regional variation.

Let's have a look at what you are paying for.

First there are the services that the funeral director provides, some of which can be omitted. The most notable are:

- the supply of a coffin

- professional charges (e.g. administration, advice)

- removal and care of body

- provision of a hearse for the funeral

- provision of a limousine for mourners

- coffin bearers

- visits to the chapel of rest

- embalming.

Then there are the services provided by third parties, which are usually described as disbursements. Funeral directors pay these fees on your behalf and add them to their bill. These would include – in the case of a cremation:

- fee to the crematorium for cremation

- fee for funeral service officiant

- cremation certificates

- funeral wreaths or flowers

- press notices

- printed funeral service cards or sheets

- organist's fees

- verger's fees (if a church service is held)

- listing of mourners.

If the deceased is to be buried rather than cremated there would be the cost of a burial site, unless there is a family plot available, and a fee for digging the grave.

Some of these services are discretionary. One piece of welcome news is that many of these items are free of Value Added Tax.

In order to avoid nasty surprises you should ask for a fully itemised written estimate from the funeral director before you proceed further. Many funeral directors do this as a matter of course and may well ask you to sign the estimate in order to approve the expenditure.

Remember that an estimate is just an estimate, and if you feel the price is too high, you can negotiate. You could save on costs, for instance, by having a less expensive coffin or cutting out the funeral car for the chief mourners. Once the funeral has taken place you are not in a position to quibble over the payment unless you have a complaint about the way the funeral has been conducted.

WHAT IS A BASIC FUNERAL?

Funeral directors belonging to the two trade associations mentioned in this chapter can offer a funeral without the trimmings provided you clearly specify from the beginning that this is what you want. This normally consists of:

◆ the collection of the deceased from the place of death (normally up to ten miles)

◆ the care of the deceased at the director's premises

◆ the supply of a simple wooden coffin

◆ a hearse to convey the deceased to the local crematorium or cemetery

◆ arrangements for the funeral and cremation/burial.

Fees for services from other providers, such as the crematorium, cemetery, church and funeral officiant have to be added on to the funeral director's costs.

ITEMISING THE COSTS

To help you decide what services you need from the funeral director, let us look at the individual items on offer.

The coffin

Most funeral directors offer a range of wooden coffins varying in quality and price to choose from. A cheaper and more ecologically friendly alternative is a cardboard coffin, but care needs to be taken that it is strong enough for the purpose and will not be affected by rain. Bamboo or wicker coffins, body bags and shrouds are also used, but it is important to check if the cemetery or crematorium is able to handle these. The funeral director should be able to advise.

Professional charges

These cover a variety of services, including an initial consultation and advice, liaising with the burial or crematorium authorities, obtaining and dealing with the necessary forms. Some firms also offer counselling.

Removal and care of the body

This tends to be a standard charge, but extra charges may be incurred if the body is taken away outside normal office hours. Normally the body is stored in a place where it cannot deteriorate and it is not embalmed unless this is specifically asked for. If anyone wishes to view the body at the funeral director's chapel of rest this may incur an additional fee.

Embalming

This method of preserving the body is not particularly common these days. However, it is essential if the body has to be preserved for a certain length of time or transported to another country.

Provision of a hearse for the funeral

Normally this will be a motorised hearse. Some undertakers can provide a funeral carriage drawn by horses, but this would work out to be an expensive option.

Limousine(s) for the chief mourners

This is the car which follows the hearse and can normally accommodate five to six people. It is not essential and the chief mourners may well wish to make their way to the funeral in their own transport like the other funeral guests. Where there are several family mourners additional cars can usually be provided at extra cost.

Coffin bearers

These are normally provided by the funeral director, but it is possible for members of the family and close friends to perform this duty. However, carrying a coffin is a skilled art and some rehearsal is vital in order to avoid accidents on the day.

Crematorium fees

Most areas have a crematorium run by the local authority, but there are also privately run crematoria. There is some variation in the costs of a cremation, but probably not enough to warrant going some distance for this service. In most cases the crematorium is attached to a cemetery or garden of rest where the ashes may be scattered free of charge. If the ashes are to be taken away in an urn, there is an extra charge.

Cremation certificates

Two doctors' certificates have to be provided before a cremation can take place, for which there is a standard charge (£110 in 2005).

Cemetery and churchyard fees

Two items have to be paid for: the plot and the digging of the grave, and there is a considerable variation in cost. In most urban areas there is no space for burials in churchyards and a cemetery has to be used. Village churchyards may well have space, but there may be restrictions as to who is eligible to be buried there. Most people opt to be buried in the local authority cemetery nearest their home, but there are a number of private cemeteries you might consider.

Burial in one's own garden is rarely an option, and in any case would require various permissions, notably from the local authority planning and environmental health departments. Bear in mind that at some future date you may wish to move residence and will have to consider whether to leave the body in situ or have it exhumed and moved to your new address (for which a Home Office licence will be required).

THE GREEN OPTION

Burial grounds in woodlands or nature reserves are becoming increasingly popular with the ecologically minded. The first one opened in the 1990s and currently there are about 200 listed in *The Natural Death Handbook* published by the Natural Death Centre.

Many of these burial grounds are privately run and do not normally have any permanent memorials, such as gravestones, as cemeteries do. Most faiths appear sympathetic to the principle of woodland burials. The Anglican Church even has a woodland burial ground of its own in Cambridgeshire, and it is likely that others will follow suit over the next few years.

An eco-friendly alternative to cremation, called promession, may become available in the future, whereby the body is not burned, but dipped in cold liquid nitrogen which causes the body to crumble away.

Fees for the funeral service

Fees are payable to the officiant at the funeral service, the organist and the verger (if the service is held in a church). In exceptional circumstances some of these fees might be waived.

Funeral Service cards

These are printed sheets with the order of service and often the words of the hymns to be sung. These are not absolutely essential as most places of worship and cemetery chapels will have funeral service books. However, it is a nice idea for people to have something to take away as a memento of the funeral service. Any spare copies left over could be sent to friends and relations who are unable to attend the funeral.

Listing of mourners

Many funeral directors can provide a person who takes the names of the people attending the funeral as they arrive. The chief mourners will be too preoccupied during the funeral to take note of who has come, and if the funeral attracts a large number of people, a list of them can be extremely useful.

Flowers

Floral wreaths and bouquets can either be ordered through the funeral director or direct from a florist, and there are usually a wide selection of packages on offer. Most florists will include delivery of the flowers direct to the funeral director's premises in the cost.

INSTRUCTING THE FUNERAL DIRECTOR

Most funeral directors are helpful and sympathetic in sorting out the arrangements, but it is wrong to leave all the arrangements to them. To get the best out of them the next of kin (or whoever is in charge) need to formulate a clear idea of their requirements and then issue clear instructions.

To clarify matters ask yourself the following questions and write down the answers.

♦ How much do you want to pay? (If you want a no-frills basic funeral you need to stipulate this from the outset.)

♦ When and where do you want the funeral to take place?

♦ Who do you want to conduct it?

♦ Where should the hearse leave from?

♦ Is there a special route you would like the funeral procession to take?

♦ How many mourners will need transport?

♦ What kind of coffin do you want?

◆ In case of a burial, where is the body to be buried? (If the body is to be buried in a family tomb or grave, precise instructions need to be given.)

As I indicated at the beginning of this section, it is not strictly speaking necessary to employ a funeral director and some people opt to arrange everything themselves. Most cemeteries are prepared to accommodate DIY funerals. However, doing it yourself can involve a good deal of time and careful planning is required in order to avoid any hitches. Generally speaking, most people are happy to entrust the arrangements to professionals at what can be a particularly stressful time.

DIY FUNERALS

Although most people prefer to use funeral directors, it is perfectly possible to make all the funeral arrangements by yourself, as the following example shows.

A PERSONAL EXPERIENCE

When a friend of his died in a hospice MC was anxious to cut down on funeral expenses so that there would be money left over from the estate to make a donation to the hospice. Someone suggested he should do all the funeral arrangements himself, so he contacted the hospital mortuary where the body was being kept after the post-mortem. The doctor who had conducted the examination said that the body could be kept there for up to two weeks until the cremation was organised.

MC then obtained cremation forms signed by the doctor and the doctor at the hospice, took them to the local crematorium together with the green form issued by the Registrar, fixed a date and time for the cremation and paid the cremation fee. He then found a funeral director who would supply him with a coffin, and gave him the full name and date of birth and death of the deceased which would be engraved on the lid of the coffin for identification purposes. He then made arrangements to hire a van for the funeral from a car hire firm.

On the day of the cremation MC loaded the coffin into the van and took it to the mortuary where the body was placed in it. On arrival at the crematorium he and a friend carried the coffin – with some difficulty – into the chapel for a brief taped service, at the end of which the coffin disappeared from view. The following working day, armed with authorisation from the crematorium office, he collected the ashes in a container from the crematorium and later took them to Ireland to be scattered in a churchyard there.

Most of the people he encountered were helpful and friendly and – even more important – the savings meant that he could make a substantial donation to the hospice.

(A fuller account of MC's experiences appear in the book *Cold Comfort* under the title *A Worthwhile Undertaking*.)

For further advice on DIY funerals, including coffin suppliers, cemeteries and crematoria, you should consult the Natural Death Centre or the handbook it publishes.

GIVING NOTIFICATION OF THE FUNERAL

Normally a funeral takes place within a week of a person's death, though it may take place later if, for example, a post mortem is needed, or one or more of the chief mourners is currently out of the country.

Relations or close friends who have indicated a wish to attend the funeral will need to be contacted. Nowadays the news is more likely to be communicated by phone or email, but if there is enough time it is quite a nice idea to send a note through the post, perhaps with a sketch map showing where the funeral is going to take place if they are unfamiliar with the area.

In order to convey news of the death and the funeral to the world at large, it is customary to place an announcement in one or two newspapers along the lines of the examples given in this book. If you need advice on the wording of the announcement, the classified department of the newspaper concerned, or the funeral director, will be able to help.

You would normally put a death announcement in a newspaper circulating in the locality where the deceased lived or used to live (see Figure 8). If the deceased was known nationally, a death notice could be placed in one or more of the national dailies, but this will be more expensive. The funeral director will be able to make the arrangements for you. If you contact the paper or papers yourself, you will be expected to produce a copy of the death certificate before the details can be published.

If the deceased was well known in the local community, it is a good idea to inform the newsroom of the local newspaper, which may wish to report the death or publish an obituary. If you can provide any details of the deceased's life, or can put

---

David Trelawney Ash
of Shakespeare Road, Milton
died peacefully on 18th February 200X
aged 90 years.
A loving and devoted husband to Angela,
a much loved father to Rachel and Donald,
and grandfather to Daphne, Emily and Rupert.
The funeral will take place at
St George's Parish Church, Milton
on Friday 28th February at 2 pm.
Family flowers only.
Donations in memory of David for the St Agnes' Hospice may be sent to Bacon and Spenser, Funeral Directors, 7 Jonson Row, Rochester RR1 7SY. Tel: 01234 567890.

ASH, David Trelawney died at Milton, Kent on 18th February aged 90. Funeral at Milton Parish Church, Kent on 28th February at 2 pm.

Figure 8. Specimen death announcements.

the editor in touch with someone who can, this will reduce the potential for errors.

(4)

Arranging a Funeral

Over the years I have attended all kinds of funerals and memorial services – traditional Christian, Quaker, Spiritualist, Humanist and Chinese – and also had a hand in organising one or two. Although their aims were similar, the differences between the ceremonies were striking. Some were uplifting; others were very conventional; some of them were deeply moving; others were exhilarating. One or two held me spellbound as I gleaned a number of unexpected facts about the deceased's life. Some worked well; others left me feeling disappointed.

Why the differences? In the case of the funerals which disappointed me, some element was lacking and it felt as if little, if any, thought had been given to them. This is not to decry the efforts of the people in charge of the arrangements, for I recognise that anyone who has just suffered a bereavement can be so overwhelmed that some of the niceties get overlooked. This is a pity. Funerals should be planned with care, and this chapter is designed to offer you some ideas on how to make a funeral memorable.

WHAT KIND OF FUNERAL?

The deceased may well have left instructions as to what kind of funeral he or she would like, whether they wish to be buried or cremated and where. These instructions may be included in the will or may have been confided to a close relative or family friend. However, as I have already mentioned, the ultimate decisions will normally be in the hands of the next of kin or the executor.

Clearly, the deceased's instructions should be respected as far as possible, but if he or she has died in Australia and requested burial in the UK, the expense of transporting a body thousands of miles may call for a rethink. This would be a matter for the closest relations to discuss among themselves and come to a reasonable compromise.

Many funerals in the UK have a Christian orientation unless the organisers specify otherwise. One consequence of this is that cemetery chapels have service books which have a liturgy (prayers and hymns) approved by the major Christian denominations.

Not that all Christian faiths will use them. A funeral held in accordance with the traditions of the Society of Friends, for instance, may have no liturgy whatsoever, but will consist of moments of quiet contemplation interrupted by prayers and tributes by members of the congregation.

If the deceased was a non-believer, a religious ceremony might be considered inappropriate. One very satisfactory way of dealing with such a situation is to have a Humanist funeral, as the actor Ronnie Barker did. The aim of the service is to celebrate the deceased's life rather than commit their soul to the hereafter and a trained officiant from the British Humanist Association or sister organisations can be engaged to conduct the ceremony in much the same way as a clergyman would. You can find out more from the Association's website or the book *Funerals without God*.

Cemetery chapels are multi-purpose and cater for all kinds of funerals – not only those of the mainstream religions. But it is perfectly acceptable to have a ceremony elsewhere – at home or by the graveside, for instance. A Chinese funeral I attended was held in the open air – initially outside the deceased's home and later in the cemetery. Some people may prefer to dispense with a funeral service altogether.

The important thing, if you are employing funeral directors, is to communicate your precise requirements to them as early as possible.

WHEN AND WHERE?

Many people settle for a simple ceremony at the local cemetery chapel, especially if the body is to be cremated. Many of these are fine buildings in pleasant settings and very suitable for the purpose.

The main disadvantage is that at certain times of the year some of these venues get very busy and in their efforts to cope with the daily throughput the authorities restrict the length of time you can spend there. Many allocate half an hour or less to each funeral, though a longer slot may be possible on payment of an additional fee. You may also have little choice in the timing of the funeral.

An alternative is to have the funeral in a church, synagogue, temple or mosque, depending on the religion of the deceased, where there is less likely to be any time limitation. Usually there is more flexibility as to the timing of the ceremony, too. If the deceased has had a close relationship with one of these institutions, the authorities will doubtless go out of their way to be accommodating.

Lapsed Christians may feel they have no option but to settle for the cemetery chapel. In fact, you have a right to a funeral in your local parish church, even if you are not a regular worshipper there.

Whatever you decide, you should inform the funeral director of your preferences regarding venue and date. You may also suggest someone to officiate at the service, which could be the local parish priest, an elder from the deceased's congregation, an officiant from the Humanist Society, a family friend or even the spouse or a child of the deceased. At one funeral I attended it was the husband of the deceased who conducted the (Humanist) funeral with great reverence and aplomb. At another the son of the deceased (a clergyman) gave the address while the service was conducted by a clergyman from the locality.

In some cases the deceased is remembered in two separate services: a small family funeral in the cemetery chapel followed (or preceded) by a memorial service at his former place of worship which is open to the wider public.

THE PERSONAL TOUCH

I have to admit to having a horror of attending funerals in cemetery chapels in winter, no matter how welcoming the staff try to make them. We therefore chose to have our mother's funeral in a church with which she had a long association in the town centre. As an added bonus we were able to call on the services of a clergyman whom she had known for many years. Although the body was destined for cremation, the committal was performed at the church door, which removed the need for any of the mourners to go to the crematorium for the final rites.

PLANNING THE FUNERAL SERVICE

As already mentioned, funerals can take many forms or can be dispensed with altogether. A funeral or memorial service is, in effect, a person's last public appearance on this earth and deserves to be accorded some importance and dignity.

In Christian practice the idea behind the funeral is to commit the dead to the afterlife, but in modern times its scope has been extended to be a service of thanksgiving for the life of the person who has passed on.

Some of the most moving funerals I have attended have attempted to reflect the nature and qualities of that person, and a great deal of thought had been given by those who knew the deceased as to how this could be best expressed.

Where possible the officiant will wish to discuss the details of the service with you beforehand and make suggestions as to the form it might take. However, you and others who were close to the deceased should feel at liberty to offer ideas of your own. Topics for consideration follow:

Music

It is customary, though not obligatory, to have music at the beginning and end of the funeral service and even during it. Most people are happy to leave the choice of music to the organist's discretion, which is quite likely to include some of the suggestions in this book (see Figure 9).

However, there is no reason why some of the deceased's favourite music should not be played. Most cemetery chapels have facilities for playing tapes and CDs, and if you can provide the funeral director or the chapel authorities with the recordings they can do the rest. The music needs to be chosen with care. For instance, the theme from *Chariots of Fire* may not be the most appropriate choice as the coffin containing the deceased heads off for cremation.

Bach: *Jesu, Joy of Man's Desiring*
Bach: *Sheep May Safely Graze*
Barber: *Adagio for Strings*
Beethoven: *Ode to Joy (from Ninth Symphony)*
Chopin: *Funeral March (from Piano Sonata in B flat)*
Elgar: *Nimrod (from The Enigma Variations)*
Fauré: *Pie Jesu (from Requiem)*
Handel: *Dead March (from Saul)*
Handel: *I Know that My Redeemer Liveth (from The Messiah)*
Mahler: *Larghetto (from Fifth Symphony)*
Mendelssohn: *Song without Words, Opus 62, No 3*
Purcell: *Dido's Lament (from Dido and Aeneas)*
Ravel: *Pavane for a Dead Princess*

Figure 9. Music for a funeral.

My own preference is for live music, but this does not have to be confined to organ music. At one funeral I attended a young relative of the deceased played a violin solo; at another, for the writer and broadcaster Humphrey Carpenter, a jazz band played the congregation in and out of the church – a lively way of reflecting one of the deceased's many interests.

Hymns

If the funeral is to be a Christian one, it is a good idea to have some hymns which are familiar to the congregation. If the service is to be in church three or four will be possible, but in many cemetery chapels where less than 30 minutes is allocated for the ceremony if you have more than two hymns the ceremony is likely to overrrun.

When choosing the hymns it is a good idea to ask around to find out if the deceased had any favourite hymns or expressed any preference before their death. Or you may have hymns in

Abide with me	Love divine, all loves excelling
All people that on earth do dwell	Make me a channel of Thy peace
All things bright and beautiful	Mine eyes have seen the glory
Amazing grace	Now thank we all our God
Be still, my soul	Now the day is over
Dear Lord and Father of mankind	O God, our help in ages past
Guide me, O thou great Redeemer	Onward, Christian soldiers
Immortal, invisible God only wise	The day Thou gavest, Lord, is ended
In heavenly love abiding	The King of Love my shepherd is
Just as I am	The Lord's my shepherd
Lead, kindly light	The old rugged cross
Lead us, heavenly Father, lead us	Thine be the glory, risen conquering son
Lord of all hopefulness	

Figure 10. Hymns suitable for a funeral.

mind which remind you of the deceased. Figure 10 lists some of the more popular ones.

Readings

If the funeral is to be a Christian one it is customary to have a reading from the Bible, though you do not need to confine yourself to Biblical texts. This is a good way to bring in other people to participate in the service.

Poems and other devotional texts may also be suitable for both religious and secular funerals, but they do not have to be religious. A poem or passage on a secular theme by the deceased's favourite writer could also be chosen.

The bibliography in this book lists a number of anthologies of suitable material which are obtainable from public libraries and bookshops. Nigel Collins' book *Seasons of Life*, for instance, features readings suitable for a Humanist funeral.

You can also find poems and prose on the internet using a search engine (e.g. Google) and typing in the words Funeral Readings. Figure 11 offers some suggestions and both the funeral director or funeral officiant will also be able to recommend passages if you have nothing particular in mind.

A tribute or eulogy

Normally part of the service is devoted to a description of the deceased's life and achievements. Sometimes a family member or friend of the deceased does the tribute. However this can be an ordeal for the person or persons concerned, and I can recall instances where the person giving the tribute broke down and had difficulty in completing the eulogy.

One way out of the difficulty is to have the eulogy incorporated into the address given by the person conducting the service. In this case you will need to furnish him or her with the person's CV and other relevant details. An alternative is to write down an account of the person's life to be read out, as I did for my mother's funeral.

A tribute does not have to be a grandiose affair, nor does it have to be unduly sad. A simple narration of the deceased's life with its significant events (education, marriage, employment, etc) and a description of his or her more endearing characteristics will usually suffice. Alternatively you could take certain aspects of the deaceased's life or personality and build the tribute around that. The booklet *How to write a*

Biblical readings

Psalm 23 The Lord is my shepherd

Psalm 90 Lord, Thou has been our dwelling-place

Psalm 103: 8–22 The Lord is merciful and gracious

Psalm 121 I will lift up mine eyes unto the hills

Psalm 130 Out of the depths I cry unto Thee, O Lord

Proverbs 31: 10–31 Who can find a virtuous woman (for the death of a wife or mother)

Ecclesiastes 3: 1–8: To everything there is a season

Matthew 5: 1–12 The Beatitudes

John 6: 35–40 And Jesus said unto them: I am the Bread of Life

John 14, verses 1–6 Let not your heart be troubled

Romans 8: 31–39 If God is for us, who can be against us

Romans 14: 7–12 For none of us liveth to himself

1 Corinthians 13: 1–13 Though I speak with the tongues on men and of angels

1 Corinthians 15: 20–26 Now is Christ risen from the dead

1 Corinthians 15: 51–57 Behold I show you a mystery

2 Corinthians 4: 7–18 But we have this treasure in earthen vessels

1 Thessalonians 4, verses 13–18 But I would not have you be ignorant

Revelation 21: 1–7; 22: 1–5 Then I saw a new heaven and a new earth

Poetry

And Death shall have no dominion Dylan Thomas

Death, be not proud John Donne

Do not go gentle into that good night Dylan Thomas

Do not stand at my grave and weep Mary Frye

Epitaph on a friend Robert Burns

Farewell to thee, but not farewell Anne Bronte

Fear no more the heat of the sun Shakespeare (*Cymbeline*)

He has outsoar'd the shadow of our night Shelley (*Adonais*)

Like as the waves make towards the pebbled shore Shakespeare (*Sonnet 60*)

Music, when sweet voices die Shelley

O may I join the choir invisible George Eliot

Remember me when I am gone away Christina Rossetti

Sleep, my body, sleep, my ghost Louis MacNiece

When I am dead, my dearest Christina Rossetti

You can shed tears that he has gone Anon

The full version of many of the prose extracts and poems suggested above can also be found on the internet using a search engine and typing in the first few words.

Figure 11. Readings and poems suitable for a funeral.

Eulogy (see bibliography) offers some useful tips, and Figure 12 offers specimen tributes.

BEFORE THE FUNERAL

The tendency is to dress conservatively as a token of respect for the dead. Women wear black dresses and sometimes black hats, while men opt for black or dark suits and perhaps a black or darkish tie. The tradition of wearing a black arm band is hardly observed these days, but at Chinese funerals it is quite common for mourners to wear white arm bands. In some situations more casual forms of dress may be acceptable – particularly in the case of someone who died young.

Usually the close family members assemble at the deceased's house on the day of the funeral to await the arrival of the hearse containing the coffin and the funeral conductor. The latter, who is normally dressed in a black frock coat, will explain the procedures.

At the appointed time the hearse leaves with a driver and the funeral conductor. This is followed by the funeral party, either in a funeral car provided (or hired in) by the funeral director to the funeral venue or their own transport. Most people attending the funeral will make their own way there, but others may wish to form part of the funeral cortege.

THE FUNERAL ITSELF

On arrival at the place of the funeral the funeral conductor leads the procession, followed by the coffin carried by bearers,

A Tribute to Phoebe Seymour by her son Gerald

We are here today to pay our repects to my mother Phoebe who passed away last week after a mercifully short illness. Although we think of her as a Lincolnshire lass she was actually born in Birmingham on 6th May 1925, the daughter of Gordon and Dorothy Seymour and sister to Uncle Frank and Auntie Georgina, who are sadly no longer with us.

She moved to Rosewood with her family in 1930 and later attended Rosewood Grammar School for Girls where she developed a passion for hockey and acting. By the time she finished school, war had broken out and she enrolled to train as a nurse at the Hollybush Royal Infirmary. Sadly her father was killed in action in Northern France in 1944, and was sadly missed.

However at the end of the 1940s another man entered her life – Oliver Seymour – whom she married in 1950. As one of the offspring of that marriage I can vouch for the fact that the 33 years they spent together were very happy ones, and nobody could wish for a kinder mum and dad.

Later she was to return to nursing and developed other interests such as choral singing, helping at the local hospice and with Help the Aged. She also fulfilled a lifetime's ambition in obtaining a degree in biology from the Open University.

When she was widowed in 1983 she moved to Bushley to be closer to my sister Debbie. Here she developed a wide range of interests, including Bushley Readers' Circle and working as a voluntary curator at the local museum.

She was a lady who was always active and wanted to make a contribution to society. She was very proud of her family and took a particular interest in the exploits of her grandchildren, her nieces and nephews. We shall all miss her very much indeed.

A Tribute to Phoebe Seymour by her daughter Deborah Spruce

Since my mother Phoebe Seymour died last week I and the family have been overwhelmed with tributes from people from all walks of life which lightened our sorrow and opened our eyes to some aspects of her life that we knew little about.

I shall always remember her as a devoted mother who did not spare herself in making our home life as happy and pleasant as possible. However, she was always very ambitious for me and my brother Gerald and could be very strict at times. I remember once getting a stern ticking off from her when I sloped off to play rounders when I should have been doing my homework, but it was all for a good cause and later we came to appreciate the sense of order she brought to our lives.

She was also an excellent nurse, by all accounts. My uncle Frank insisted that she had the ability to become a fully fledged doctor, but instead she found her vocation in nursing working for a number of years, first in Bristol, then Lincolnshire and finally at the Willows Nursing Home in Appletree. She was a person who cared deeply for her patients and she seemed to bring a ray of sunshine into their lives.

One of the most endearing aspects about her was that she was incredibly active and interested in everything. She had been an enthusiastic hockey player and amateur actress in her youth. Then she took to dancing and swept my father off his feet. Choral singing was another of her passions. After my father died we expected her to lead a quieter life. But no. She became one of the leading lights of Bushley Readers' Circle, and if you happened to drop into the Bushley Museum she would grab hold of you and subject you to a 30-minute guided tour.

We all have such happy memories of Phoebe Seymour, and how wonderful it is that so many people have turned out today to pay their respects to someone who was caring, hard working and great fun to have around. She really did bring a ray of sunshine into the lives of all of us.

Figure 12. Specimen tributes.

the funeral officiant and the chief mourners. The coffin is placed in position and the chief mourners normally take their places in seats on the right at the front.

At church funerals and some that take place in cemetery chapels the congregation is already seated when the procession enters. At others the congregation file in after the chief mourners and take their seats as directed by the funeral conductor.

If this is a cremation, at the end of the funeral the coffin normally disappears from view as the officiant says the committal, often to the accompaniment of music. The congregation wait for the chief mourners to leave and then follow them out of the venue. A plate is sometimes left by the door for any donations people care to make.

If the body is to be buried, the family mourners follow the coffin and officiant out of the chapel or church to the final burial place in the cemetery or churchyard. The congregation stand in a circle at the graveside, the coffin is lowered into the grave and the officiant says the prayers of committal. Sometimes the mourners sprinkle earth over the coffin.

Many variations are, of course, possible. Sometimes the funeral consists only of a graveside ceremony; at other funerals the coffin is already in place when the mourners arrive. The service may be short, simple and sweet or, in the case of a Christian funeral, could also incorporate the eucharist or a mass.

AFTER THE FUNERAL

The ceremony over, the chief mourners and the officiant greet the visitors and exchange brief words with them. If a reception has been arranged you may wish to issue an invitation to anyone present.

It is always a good idea to arrange some kind of get-together after the funeral, particularly if a number of those attending have come from some distance. Although you may dread the experience of meeting large numbers of people during what can be a difficult time, it may well turn out to be an enjoyable, heart-warming occasion.

Receptions do not have to be elaborate affairs. Tea and sandwiches in someone's home or a church hall will suffice. However, offering hospitality after a funeral can be time-consuming and it is really the next of kin's responsibility to circulate and talk to the guests, some of whom you may not have seen for a long time.

For this reason you might consider entrusting the catering to friends or a catering company, or holding the reception in a hotel or restaurant close to the place where the funeral has taken place. Any expenditure incurred is an allowable expense against the deceased's estate.

FINISHING ON A HIGH NOTE

My mother had left strict instructions for a cooked lunch to be organised in her favourite restaurant for everyone attending her funeral. The restaurant put on a buffet lunch which was much appreciated by those present, since it was a particularly dull and chilly winter's day. The food and wine flowed freely and so did the conversation, and everyone left in high spirits.

5

Winding Up the Deceased's Affairs

Once the funeral is out of the way it is time to get down to sorting out the deceased's affairs – a process which can take months, even years, depending on how complicated they are.

The first task for the next of kin (or whoever has been sorting things out thus far) is to find out who is responsible for doing this. If the deceased has made a will, everyone named as an executor of the will should be contacted at the earliest possible opportunity. As the personal representatives of the deceased they are legally responsible for dealing with the assets of the estate – a task which involves settling outstanding bills and distributing what remains of the estate to the heirs.

If there are no executors, or none of them is able or willing to execute the will, the task falls to the beneficiary of the residue of the estate (or the sole beneficiary) who becomes the administrator of the will. (The residue is what is left of the estate after the bills have been paid and bequests made.)

In Scotland different terminology is used. The equivalent of an executor is the executor nominate while an administrator of a will is the executor dative.

AN UNWILLING EXECUTOR

Two executors were named in my father's will, but by the time of his death 40 years later one of these was dead and the other, being well advanced in years, did not want the reponsibility of dealing with the will. He therefore renounced the right to act as the executor and so responsibility for administering the estate was transferred to my father's sole beneficiary, my mother, who applied not for probate, but for letters of administration.

WHAT HAPPENS IF THERE IS NO WILL?

Six people out of every ten die without having made a will. In other words they die intestate, and responsibility for administering the estate would normally fall to the deceased's next of kin in the following order of precedence:

1 Lawful husband or wife

2 Sons or daughters (but not step-children)

3 Parents

4 Brothers or sisters

5 Grandparents

6 Uncles or aunts

If people in categories 4 and 6 are dead, nephews, nieces and cousins of the deceased become eligible to apply for letters of administration. In Scotland different rules apply.

If the deceased has not given any officially recognised guidelines as to who should benefit from their estate in the form of a will, it has to be distributed according to the rules of intestacy (see Figure 1, page 7). This sets down clear guidelines as to who should inherit and what proportion of the estate they should inherit after liabilities have been taken care of. If you were permanently resident outside of England and Wales when you died, your estate will be subject to the intestacy rules of the country in question.

PROVING THE WILL

Whether there is a will or not, the people administering the estate need to obtain a *Grant of Representation* from the Probate Registry before they can begin (see Figure 13). The *Grant of Representation* is a legal document which authorises a person or persons to collect the money and assets of the deceased, pay outstanding bills and distribute the estate. Banks, insurance companies and other organisations holding the deceased's money and assets will normally wish to see the document before they will release any of the assets.

Is it really necessary to apply for probate? In most cases, yes, but there are two possible exceptions:

Probate Application Form - PA1

Please use **BLOCK CAPITALS**

Name of deceased

Forenames

Surname

Please state where you wish to be interviewed (see enclosed PA4). You can be interviewed at the Controlling Probate Registry of your choice or at one of its interview venues. Please also specify dates when you will **not** be available for interview.

Please read the following questions and PA2 booklet 'How to obtain probate' carefully before filling in this form. Please also refer to the Guidance Notes enclosed where an item is marked *.

PLEASE COMPLETE ALL SECTIONS.

This column is for official use

Section A: The Will / Codicil

*A1 Did the deceased leave a will/codicil? *(Note: These may not necessarily be formal documents. If the answer to question 1 is Yes, you must enclose the **original** document(s) with your application.)*

Will		Codicil	
Yes ☐	No ☐	Yes ☐	No ☐

If **No** to both questions, please go to Section B

Date of will/codicil

A2 Is there anyone under 18 years old who receives anything in the will/codicil?

Yes ☐   No ☐

A3 Are there any executors named in the will/codicil?

Yes ☐   No ☐

*A4 Give the names of those executors who are **not** applying and the reasons why. Please see attached Guidance Notes. **All** executors **must** be accounted for.

Full names	Reason A,B,C,D,E

A = Pre-deceased
B = Died after the deceased
C = Power Reserved
D = Renunciation
E = Power of Attorney

*B1 - B6

Please refer to the Guidance Notes.

Sections B1 - B4 must be completed in all cases.

Please state the **number** of relatives of the deceased in categories B1 - B4.

If there are no relatives in a particular category, write 'nil' in each box and move onto the next category.

Note: Sections B5 and B6 only need to be completed if the deceased had no relatives in Section B1 - B4.

Section B: Relatives of the deceased

Number of relatives (if none, write nil)	Under 18	Over 18
B1 Surviving **lawful** husband or wife or surviving **lawful** civil partner		
B2a Sons or daughters who survived the deceased		
b Sons or daughters who did **not** survive the deceased		
c Children of person(s) indicated at '2b' **only** who survived the deceased *		
B3 Parents who survived the deceased		
B4a Brothers or sisters who survived the deceased		
b Brothers or sisters who did **not** survive the deceased		
c Children of person(s) indicated at '4b' **only** who survived the deceased *		
B5 Grandparents who survived the deceased		
B6a Uncles or aunts who survived the deceased		
b Uncles or aunts who did **not** survive the deceased		
c Children of person(s) indicated at '6b' **only** who survived the deceased *		

PA1 - Probate Application Form (02.06)

HMCS

Figure 13. Probate application form.

		Section C: Details of applicant(s)	This column is for official use

Please note that the grant will normally be sent to the first applicant. Any applicant named will be required to attend an interview. It is, however, usually only necessary for one person to apply (please see PA2 booklet, page 3).

C1 Title — Mr ☐ Mrs ☐ Miss ☐ Ms ☐ Other ☐ — I.T.W.C

C2 Forenames

C3 Surname

C4 Address

Postcode:

C5 Telephone number — Home / Work

C6 Occupation

C7 Are you related to the deceased? — Yes ☐ No ☐

If Yes, what is your relationship? — Relationship:

C8 If there are any other applicants, up to a maximum of three, give their details. (Note: **All** applicants named in Sections C1 and C8 must attend an interview.)

Details of other applicants who wish to be named in the grant of representation. (Please give details as C1 to C7.)

C9 Name and address of any surviving lawful husband or wife/civil partner of the deceased, unless stated above.

Postcode:

*C10 If you are applying as an attorney on behalf of the person entitled to the grant, please state their name, address and capacity in which they are entitled (e.g. relationship to the deceased).

Postcode:

Relationship:

C10a Has the person named in section C10 signed an Enduring Power of Attorney? — Yes ☐ No ☐

C10b If Yes, has it been registered with the Public Guardianship Office? — Yes ☐ No ☐

Figure 13. *Continued.*

	Section D: Details of the deceased	This column is for official use
*D1 Forenames		
*D2 Surname		True name
*D3 Did the deceased hold any assets (**excluding joint assets**) in another name?	Yes ☐ No ☐	Alias
*D4 If Yes, what are the assets?		
And in what name(s) are they held?		
D5 Last permanent address of the deceased.		Address
	Postcode:	
D6 Date of birth		
D7 Date of death	Age:	D/C district and No.
D8 Was England and Wales the permanent home of the deceased? If No, please specify the deceased's permanent home.	Yes ☐ No ☐	L.S.A. D.B.F.
*D9 Tick the last **legal** marital or civil partnership status of the deceased, and give dates where appropriate.	Bachelor/Spinster ☐ Widow/Widower ☐ Surviving Civil Partner ☐ Married ☐ Date: Civil Partnership ☐ Date: Divorced ☐ Date: Civil Partnership dissolved ☐ Date: Judicially separated ☐ Date:	
Note: These documents (✦) may usually be obtained from the Court which processed the divorce/dissolution of civil partnership/separation.	(If the deceased did **not** leave a will, please enclose official copy✦ of the Decree Absolute/Decree of Dissolution of Civil Partnership/Decree of Judicial Separation (as applicable))	
Note: You do not need to complete questions D10 and D11 if you are applying as executor.		
*D10 Was the deceased legally adopted?	Yes ☐ No ☐	
*D11 Has any relative of the deceased been legally adopted? (If Yes, give name and relationship to deceased.)	Yes ☐ No ☐ Name: Relationship:	

D12 *Answer this section* **only** *if the deceased died* **before 4th April 1988 or left a will or codicil dated before that date**.

D12a Was the deceased illegitimate?	Yes ☐ No ☐	
D12b Did the deceased leave any illegitimate sons or daughters?	Yes ☐ No ☐	
D12c Did the deceased have any illegitimate sons or daughters who died leaving children of their own?	Yes ☐ No ☐	

Important - please complete the checklist overleaf before submitting your application

Figure 13. *Continued.*

Important

Checklist

Please return your forms to the probate registry which controls the interview venue at which you wish to be interviewed (see PA4) otherwise your application may be delayed.

Before sending your application, please complete this checklist to confirm that you have enclosed the following items:

1. PA1 (Probate Application Form)

2. Either IHT205 (signed by all applicants)
   or D18 (signed)
   Note: Do not enclose IHT Form 200 — **this must be sent to C.T.O.** (see PA2)

3. Original will and codicil(s), **not a photocopy**
   Note: Do **not** remove or attach anything to the will/codicil

4. Official copy of death certificate or coroner's letter, **not a photocopy**

5. Other documents as requested on PA1 — please specify

6. Please state number of official copy grants required for use in England and Wales (see PA3)

7. Please state number of official copy grants required for use **outside** England and Wales (see PA3)

   For official use only (sealed and certified)

8. Please state total amount of cheque enclosed for fee (made payable to HMCS) including cost for the number of official copy grants stated in 6 and 7 above.

   £

Note: If you do not enclose all the relevant items, your application may be delayed.

Official Use Only

Type of grant:

Power reserved to _____ [Name of executor/s]

Will message: with a codicil / and _____ codicils (delete as appropriate)

Limitation _____

Min interest   Yes / No

Life interest   Yes / No

Figures:- DNE / amounts to   Gross: £
                                    Net: £   Fee paid: £

Clearing:-

Title:-

Footnote:-

Figure 13. *Continued.*

- If the estate is held jointly and everything passes to the surviving owner.

- If the estate is very small (with no assets worth over £5,000) some organisations may release the money to you without the need for a *Grant of Representation.*

Generally speaking, it is wise to err on the side of caution and assume that you need to apply for a *Grant of Representation.* Your local probate registry can give you advice on this, and you could also call the Probate Helpline or access the relevant pages of the Court Service website.

In Scotland probate is known as confirmation. It has to be obtained at the sheriff court of the sheriffdom in which the deceased was living at the time of death.

EMPLOYING A SOLICITOR

In some wills a solicitor is named as the executor and you have no say in the matter. Otherwise the executors or administrator of the will have a choice: to administer it themselves or hand it over to a solicitor to deal with.

Administering an estate need not be complicated, provided you have sufficient time to spare, proceed methodically and take advice if there are any matters you do not understand. There can be important savings to be made if you take the DIY route, since you do not have to pay any solicitor's fees out of the estate. The booklet *How to Obtain Probate:*

A Guide for the Applicant Acting Without a Solicitor, obtainable from the Probate Registry, outlines what is involved.

There are circumstances, however, when it may be prudent to seek legal advice. Examples are where:

◆ the deceased left no will (died intestate)

◆ the will is badly worded and could give rise to differing interpretations

◆ any provisions in the will are likely to be contested

◆ you are not sure you know about all the deceased's debts

◆ the deceased has assets abroad

◆ there are business interests involved

◆ there is not enough money in the estate to pay the debts

◆ any beneficiaries are under 18 years old.

You could get advice from organisations such as the Citizens' Advice Bureau or Cruse Bereavement Care in the first instance.

INVESTING AN INHERITANCE

An uncle of mine bequeathed a proportion of his estate to his two great-grandchildren for them to inherit when they attained the age of 18. The joint executors, in their capacity as trustees, invested the money set aside for them, which appreciated in value and was paid out to the beneficiaries several years later when they attained their majority.

If you decide to enlist a solicitor and have nobody particular in mind, you should make sure you choose one with particular expertise in wills and probate law. Again the Citizens' Advice Bureau could be of help, you could look in *Yellow Pages* (in which most solicitors list their areas of expertise) or you could contact the Law Society for a list of suitably qualified solicitors in your area.

You should try to get an estimate of the solicitor's likely fees at the outset. Some may quote a flat fee, if the will is straightforward, but if it is difficult for them to estimate the amount of time involved, they will quote you an hourly rate (e.g. £100) and/or base their fee on the value of the estate (e.g. two per cent). If you are on a low income you may be able to get legal aid, but the costs will probably be recouped from the estate.

ESTABLISHING ASSETS AND LIABILITIES

Before applying for a Grant of Representation (probate) from the Probate Registry there are various matters that need to be attended to. In many ways it makes sense to get the funeral over before tackling them, but if you have the time you can start earlier.

One of the priorities must be to establish what the deceased's assets and liabilities are, as this information is needed for when the application is submitted for probate (or by the solicitor, if you plan to use one).

If the deceased was well organised (having read Chapter 1 of this book, perhaps!) they will have compiled a list of assets which also states where the relevant documents are to be found. Often they will have been kept in a safe or strong box – or perhaps lodged with the deceased's bank, solicitor or accountant.

However, it is not always that easy. Old people, in particular, have a tendency to squirrel things away in an attic or among a pile of papers at the bottom of a cupboard. Younger people, who assume that they have plenty of years before them, may not have bothered to keep any records at all. It makes sense to persist in your search or an important document may get overlooked.

OFFICIAL NOTIFICATIONS

A number of organisations in addition to the Registrar will require official notification of the death. While some of these matters can be dealt with by telephone or a personal visit, more often than not institutions will request written confirmation and a copy of the death certificate.

Where money has to be released, or assets sold or transferred, the organisations concerned will probably also want to see the Grant of Representation from the Probate Registry before they can act.

In administering my mother's affairs I opted to write letters to most of the organisations I needed to contact, and filed away copies of the letters and the replies received (see Figure 14). In this way I had a complete record of what had been done.

Stour Cottage
Avonlea
Merseyshire
19 October 200X

The Manager
Severn Building Society
Thamesmead
TH2 8HH

Dear Sir,

I am sorry to inform you that your client Arnold Matthew Tweed of Avonlea passed away on the 9th of this month. His account number was 86421 and I would be glad if you could let know how much there is in this account as I shall need to know this information when I apply for probate with the other executor of Mr Tweed's will.

Please let me know what documentation you need in order to wind up this account.

Yours sincerely,

Bernard Trent

Figure 14. Specimen official notification letter.

The list of organisations and agencies which follows does not claim to be fully comprehensive, and some may not be relevant to the deceased's affairs. If you are employing a solicitor, you should discuss which, if any, of the following matters you can deal with yourself. The more you do for yourself, the lower the legal fees will be.

Bereavement register

It is not absolutely necessary to inform this organisation when a death occurs, but doing so will remove the deceased's name from mail order databases and prevent the sending of unwanted junk mail addressed to the deceased. (See Useful Addresses.)

Bank

The bank (or banks) needs to be informed of the date that the person died.

If the account is a joint one, there is usually no problem in transferring it into the name of the surviving holder. If it is a sole account, the bank will freeze it, cancelling all standing orders or direct debits as well as any debit or credit cards linked to the account. It will ask you to destroy any bank stationery (such as cheque books and paying in slips) and any credit or debit cards.

The bank may be prepared to release the money in the account if the total estate is under a certain amount, but this will require you and other interested parties to sign an indemnity form and send a copy of the will (if one exists). Otherwise the bank will need to see the Grant of Representation when it is issued.

When approaching the bank you should ask for details of the balance held in the account. This information will be needed at a later date for the inheritance tax form. You should also check whether there are any documents or certificates kept in the bank on behalf of the deceased.

Building society
A building society will adopt a similar procedure to a bank in the case of savings accounts and ISAs.

If the deceased had a mortgage in joint names, responsibility for paying off the mortgage is transferred to the survivor. If not, the society will probably agree to suspend payments until the grant of representation comes through and will then need to discuss future arrangements. You should also check whether any insurance has been taken out which guarantees payment of the mortgage on the death of a mortgagee.

Council
Your local council will need to be informed regarding housing benefit or council tax benefit (which are normally payable if your savings and investments amount to less than £16,000). If the house is now going to be occupied by one person instead of two, a reduction of 25 per cent in council tax is due.

You should also ask for the electoral registration officer to be informed so that the deceased's name is deleted from the electoral register.

Credit card issuer

If the deceased's credit card is issued by a company other than their bank you should report the death and ask for an up-to-date statement. You should make it clear that there could be a delay in payment of the account until the grant of representation comes through.

Driver and Vehicle Licensing Agency (DVLA)

The DVLA will need to be informed of the death so that the deceased can be deleted from their records, and the driving licence should be sent back. If the deceased's car is to be off the road for some time you should make a Statutory Off Road Declaration (SORN) form V85/1 – or V11 (the vehicle licence renewal reminder). A refund may be given. Otherwise, if the ownership of the car is transferred, the vehicle registration certificate must be signed and forwarded to the DVLA or the equivalent agency in Scotland or Northern Ireland.

Electricity supplier

If the account is in the deceased's name it should be transferred to the name of the person who is going to occupy the property. If the property is not going to be lived in for a time, arrangements should be made for the meter to be read, the supply disconnected and outstanding bills sent to the deceased's personal representative.

Employer

The deceased's employer will doubtless have been informed of the death, but now is the time to check whether any unpaid salary, illness or death benefits are due, or if any company pension is payable to the estate or any surviving partner.

In the case of full-time students, the educational establishment attended should be informed.

Gas supplier

The same procedures need to be actioned as in the case of the electricity supplier.

Income tax

The relevant HM Revenue and Customs (Inland Revenue) office should be informed in writing of the death quoting, if possible, the deceased's reference number. The officers will also need to be sent a copy of the death certificate before thay can issue any rebate for overpayment of tax which may be due. Inheritance tax is dealt with separately at the end of this chapter.

If you cannot find the deceased's income tax details and the local tax office has no record, ask their former employer or, in the case of a self-employed person, try the office in the area where their business was based.

If the deceased had an accountant they should take charge of these tax matters. The leaflet IR45 *What to Do About Tax When Someone Dies* can steer you in the right direction.

Insurance

Insurance companies should be informed of the death and you should check whether they need to see a death certificate. Car insurance is not usually transferable, and the agreement will need to be terminated and any overpayment refunded to the estate. Anyone entitled to drive on the deceased's insurance policy will cease to be legally insured. House insurance is usually transferable to any person continuing to reside in the house or whoever is in charge of handling the property.

Landlord

If the tenancy agreement is in the deceased's name, and someone will continue to live in the property, a new contract will have to be agreed and signed. Usually the tenancy can be transferred without any problems if it was joint, but this is by no means automatic in other circumstances – especially if the property is owned by a local council or housing trust.

Where the deceased was the sole tenant the tenancy will need to be terminated and arrangements made to remove the deceased's possessions from the property. Any outstanding rent payments will have to wait until the Grant of Representation comes through, and the landlord will need to be informed accordingly.

Library

Library books and tickets should be returned.

Life assurance

This becomes payable on the production of a death certificate and payment will normally be made to whoever is nominated as the beneficiary. Otherwise it will be paid to whoever is administering the estate.

Medical matters

Any outstanding hospital, dental or surgery appointments should be cancelled and the reason given to the organisations concerned. Any borrowed equipment should be returned to the local hospital or family doctor's surgery.

National Savings

The relevant offices need to be informed and instructions given on payment but, as with banks, they may ask to see the Grant of Representation. Premium Bond holdings do not need to be cashed in immediately, but can be held for a further 12 months and are eligible for any prize won during this time. At the end of this period the investment is paid out to the estate.

Passport

This should be returned to the passport office which issued it.

Pensions

State pension: the Pension Service and Benefits Office should be informed either by letter or by calling at a social security office (DWP) and any payment books, cheques or cards returned. If you were in receipt of a married person's pension this will be replaced by a single person's pension. For more information refer to Leaflet NP45 *A Guide to State Retirement Pensions*. You may also be eligible for a Bereavement Payment.

Personal or company pension: the pension provider should be informed and arrangements made for any outstanding payments to be made to the estate or any surviving partner.

Social security benefits (DWP)

There are a number of benefits that a married spouse may be eligible for, details of which are available from the local social security office or Job Centre as well as Leaflet GL14 *Widowed? A Basic Guide to Benefits and Tax Credits* and Leaflet NP45 *A Guide to Bereavement Payments*. Claims must normally be made within three months of the death.

The benefits include:

◆ Bereavement Payment. This is a tax-free lump sum of £2,000 for non-pensioners.

◆ Bereavement Allowance. This is payable to non-pensioners aged over 45 for up to 52 weeks.

◆ Widowed Parent's Allowance. This is a non-means tested benefit based upon the deceased's National Insurance contributions payable for as long as the claimant is receiving Child Benefit.

◆ Incapacity Benefit. In certain circumstances if you are widowed you may now qualify for this benefit, even if you did not do so previously. (See Leaflet IB202 *Incapacity Benefit*.)

Social services department of local council

If the deceased has been getting meals on wheels, home care or day care, the social services office of the local council should be told and arrangements made for the return of any equipment.

Subscriptions

The deceased may have subscribed to a club, association, publication or charity. These would need to be informed and payments stopped. In some cases (e.g. subscription to a magazine) a refund may be due.

Sundry creditors

It may not always be possible to find out who these are until requests for payment are received. In all instances you should explain the circumstances and refer creditors to the person dealing with the estate. Under no account should anyone accept responsibility for paying any bills at this stage. Most creditors will accept that this cannot be done until the Grant of Representation comes through.

Telephone provider

If the telephone is no longer needed, arrangements should be made to have it disconnected and for an invoice to be sent to the deceased's personal representative.

Trade union or friendly society

Some of these pay out funeral benefits or other benefits to their members, so it is well worth contacting them with news and evidence of the death.

TV licensing

If the TV licence is in the deceased's name the Licensing Office at Bristol should be notified.

Water company

If the contract is with the deceased, the water company should be notified. If necessary, arrangements should be made for the supply to be turned off.

APPLYING FOR A GRANT OF REPRESENTATION

Before any payments can be made from the estate the personal representatives need to obtain a legal document called a Grant of Representation. (If you are employing a solicitor, they will do this.) This is a five stage process:

1. Obtaining the forms

You will need two forms:

- the *Probate Application Form* (PA1): see Figure 13.

- the *Return of Estate Information Form* (IHT 205): see Figure 15.

Inland Revenue
Capital Taxes

Return of estate information

Probate and inheritance tax
Helpline
0845 30 20 900

Fill in this form where the person who has died ("the deceased") had their permanent home in the United Kingdom at the date of death and the **gross value of the estate for inheritance tax**
• is less than the excepted estate limit, **or**
• is less than £1,000,000 **and** there is no inheritance tax to pay because of spouse or charity exemption **only**.

"✓"

About the person who has died

Title 1.1   Surname 1.2

Other name(s) 1.3

Date of death 1.4 / /   Marital status 1.5

Occupation 1.6   National Insurance number 1.7

Surviving relatives "✓"

Husband/Wife 1.8   Brother(s)/Sister(s) "✓" 1.9   Parent(s) "✓" 1.10

Number of children 1.11   Number of grandchildren 1.12

You should read the notes about each question in booklet IHT206 as you fill in this form. *Everyone must answer questions 2 - 8.*

About the estate

No   Yes

2. Within seven years of death did the deceased

   a. make any gifts or other transfers totalling more than £3,000 per year, other than normal birthday, festive or wedding gifts, **or**

   b. give up the right to benefit from any assets held in trust.

   *If you answer 'Yes' to either part of question 2, include the chargeable value of the gifts in box 12.1. But if this value is more than £100,000 or the assets do not qualify as 'specified transfers' (see IHT206) **stop filling in this form, you will need to fill in form IHT200 instead.***

3. On or after 18 March 1986, did the deceased make a gift where

   a. they continued to benefit from, or had some right to benefit from, or use all or part of the asset, **or**

   b. the person receiving the gift did not take full possession of it?

   *If you answer 'Yes' to either part of question 3, **stop filling in this form, you will need to fill in form IHT200 instead.***

4. Did the deceased have the right to receive the benefit from any assets held in a trust?

   If you answer 'Yes' to question 4 and the deceased
   • *was entitled to benefit from a single trust, and*
   • *the value of the assets in that trust was less than £100,000,*
   *include the value of the trust assets in box 12.2. But if the value is more than £100,000, or there is more than one trust, **stop filling in this form, you will need to fill in form IHT200 instead.***

5. Did the deceased own or benefit from any assets outside the UK?

   *If you answer 'Yes' to question 5 include the value of the overseas assets in box 12.5. But if the value of the overseas assets is more than £75,000, **stop filling in this form, you will need to fill in form IHT200 instead.***

6. Did the deceased pay premiums on any life insurance policies that were not for the deceased's own benefit or did not pay out to the estate?

   If you answer 'Yes' to question 6, you must also answer question 9.

IHT205

Figure 15. Return of estate information form.

			No	Yes
7.	Was the deceased a member of a pension scheme or did they have a personal pension policy from which they had not taken their full retirement benefits before the date of death?		☐	☐

If you answer 'Yes' to question 7, you must also answer question 10.

8. a. Was the deceased entitled to receive payments from a pension which continued to be paid after they had died (other than arrears of pension)? ☐ ☐

b. Was a lump sum payable under a pension scheme or pension policy as a result of the death? ☐ ☐

If you answer 'Yes' to question 8, see IHT206 to find out how to include the asset in section 11.

Do not answer questions 9 or 10 unless you answered 'Yes' to questions 6 or 7.

9. Within seven years of the death, did the deceased

a. pay any premium on a life insurance policy under which the benefit is payable other than to the estate, or to the spouse of the deceased, *and if so* ☐ ☐

b. did they buy an annuity at any time? ☐ ☐

*If you answer 'Yes' to question 9(a), see IHT206 to find out how to include the premiums paid on this form. If you answer 'Yes' to **both** question 9(a) & 9(b). **stop filling in this form, you will need to fill in form IHT200 instead.***

10. At a time when they were in poor health or terminally ill, did the deceased change their pension scheme or personal pension policy so as to

a. dispose of any of the benefits payable, or ☐ ☐

b. make any change to the benefits to which they were entitled? ☐ ☐

*If you answer 'Yes' to question 10(a) or 10(b). **stop filling in this form, you will need to fill in form IHT200 instead.***

11. **Deceased's own assets (including joint assets NOT passing by survivorship - see IHT206)**

- *You must include the gross value for each item below, before deduction of any exemption or relief.*
- *You must include all the assets that were part of the deceased's estate as at the date of death, ignoring any changes that may take place through an Instrument of Variation made after the death.*
- *You must make full enquiries so that you can show that the figures that you give in this form are right. If you cannot find out the value for an item, you may include your best estimate.* Tick the box to show estimates "✓"

11.1	Cash, including money in banks, building societies and National Savings	**11.1** £	☐
11.2	Household and personal goods	**11.2** £	☐
11.3	Stocks and shares quoted on the Stock Exchange	**11.3** £	☐
11.4	Stocks and shares not quoted on the Stock Exchange	**11.4** £	☐
11.5	Insurance policies, including bonuses and mortgage protection policies	**11.5** £	☐
11.6	Money owed to the person who has died	**11.6** £	☐
11.7	Partnership and business interests	**11.7** £	☐
11.8	Freehold/leasehold residence of the person who has died	**11.8** £	☐
	Address (including postcode)		
11.9	Other freehold/leasehold residential property	**11.9** £	☐
	Address (including postcode)		
11.10	Other land and buildings	**11.10** £	☐
	Address/location		
11.11	Any other assets not included above	**11.11** £	☐
	Total estate for which a grant is required (sum of boxes 11.1 to 11.11)	**A** £	

2

Figure 15. *Continued.*

12. **Other assets forming part of the estate**   *Tick the box to show estimates "✓"*

12.1 Gifts and other lifetime transfers (after deduction of exemptions)   **12.1** £

Details of gifts

12.2 Assets held in trust for the benefit of the deceased   **12.2** £

Details of trust

12.3 Share of joint assets passing automatically to the surviving joint owner   **12.3** £

Details of joint assets

12.4 Nominated assets   **12.4** £

12.5 Assets outside the United Kingdom (value in £ sterling)   **12.5** £

Total (sum of boxes 12.1 to 12.5)   **B** £

Gross estate for inheritance tax (A + B)   **C**

13. **Debts of the estate**

13.1 Funeral expenses   **13.1** £

13.2 Mortgage on a property in the sole name of the deceased   **13.2** £

13.3 Other debts owed by the deceased in the UK   **13.3** £

Total debts owing in the UK (sum of boxes 13.1 to 13.3)   **D**

13.4 Debts payable out of trust assets   **13.4** £

13.5 Share of mortgage on a property owned in joint names   **13.5** £

13.6 Share of other debts payable out of joint assets   **13.6** £

13.7 Debts owing to persons outside the UK   **13.7** £

Total of other debts (sum of boxes 13.4 to 13.7)   **E** £

Total debts (D + E)   **F** £

Net estate for inheritance tax (C - F)   **G** £

14. *Use this space to provide any other information we have asked for or you would like taken into account.*

3

Figure 15. *Continued.*

Carried Foward **G** £ _____

15. **Exemptions (you should read IHT206 before filling in this section)**

In the box below, deduct any exemption for assets passing on death to
- *the spouse of the deceased, or*
- *a UK charity or for national purposes*

Describe the extent of the exemption deducted. If for charities, etc give the name of the charity(s) or other organisation(s) benefiting. Where exemptions are deducted for particular assets, list those assets and show the amount deducted.

15.1
_____

H £ _____

Net qualifying value for excepted estates (G - H) **J** £ _____

15.2 Tax district and/or income tax reference number   [15.2] _____

If the value in box J is more than the excepted estate limit, you must fill in form IHT200.

If you find something has been left out, or if any of the figures you have given in this form change later on, you only need to tell us if, taking all the omissions and changes into account,
- the figure at box G is now higher than the inheritance tax threshold, **and**
- there are no exemptions to deduct which keep the value at box J below the inheritance tax threshold.

If, at any time, the value at box J is more than the inheritance tax threshold, you must list any new items and the items that have changed in a Corrective Account (form C4) and send it to us with a copy of this form along with a cheque for the tax that has become payable.

The issue of the grant does not mean that there is no inheritance tax due on this estate.

To the best of my/our knowledge and belief, the information I/we have given in this form is correct and complete. I/We have read and understand the statements above.

I/We understand that I/we may have to pay financial penalties if the answers to the questions or figures that I/we give in this form are wrong because of my/our fraud or negligence, OR if the estate fails to qualify as an excepted estate and I/we do not deliver a corrective account within 6 months of the failure coming to my/our notice.

	Name Address	
	Signature & Date	
	Name Address	
	Signature & Date	

Summary

Gross estate in the United Kingdom passing under Will or by intestacy	**A** £	
Debts in the United Kingdom owed by the deceased alone	**D** £	
Net estate in the United Kingdom (A - D)	**K** £	

Probate and inheritance tax Helpline 0845 30 20 900

4

Figure 15. *Continued.*

These are available from your local probate registry, the address of which you will find in the telephone directory or on the website www.courtservice. You could also call the Probate Helpline: 08453 020900.

2. Completing the forms

The Return of Estate Information Form (IHT205) has to be returned at the same time as the probate application form.

When completing the probate information form you should refer to the accompanying notes. If in section C there is more than one person applying for the Grant of Representation, the Grant will be sent to the first of the applicants. There is a helpline you can ring if you have any problems.

3. Returning the forms

The two forms need to be returned to the Probate Registry of the area where you wish to be interviewed. You will need to enclose:

◆ The original will.

◆ An official copy of the death certificate.

◆ Any other documents requested in Form PA1.

◆ A cheque to cover the cost of the grant and any official copies you require. In 2005 the fee was £130 plus £1 per copy. If the net estate is under £5,000 the £130 fee is waved but fees for the copies are payable.

GETTING IT RIGHT

When applying for probate for my mother's estate I decided to deliver the forms by hand to the local probate registry, where I asked the officer on duty to check to see that I had filled in the probate application form correctly. I also enquired how many copies of the grant I was likely to need and she suggested half a dozen. I took her advice and was pleased to find that this number was about right. I was able to write a cheque and was given a receipt straightaway.

4. Attending an interview

Assuming there are no complications with your application, within two weeks you should receive an invitation to attend an interview at the Probate Office, or one of its outposts. This is a fairly short process at which you are required to swear or affirm that the information you have given is correct. You will also have an opportunity to ask questions. If there is more than one executor it is only necessary for one of them to attend.

5. Receiving the Grant of Representation

After a few weeks you will receive a *Grant of Representation* through the post, together with any extra copies ordered and a copy of the will. The original will is retained by the Probate Registry for official records.

Now you are in a position to contact organisations holding the deceased's money or property which will release these assets when they have seen an official copy of the Grant.

COMPLETING THE INHERITANCE TAX FORM

The *Return of Estate Information Form*, as it is called, will come with the probate application form and will have to be completed and sent back to the Probate Registry at the same time as the PA1. They will pass this particular form on to HM Customs and Revenue Capital Taxes Office.

Form IHT205 needs to completed if the total value of the estate (after exemptions) falls below the Inheritance Tax threshold (£285,000 in 2006/7, £300,000 in 2007/8, £312,000 in 2008/9 and £325,000 in 2009/10), as 94 per cent of all estates currently escape IHT.

The form needs to be completed carefully with reference to the very comprehensive booklet of instructions which accompany it. It is a good idea to make a photocopy of it to practise on before filling in the final copy.

If when answering questions 2–10 the answer is Yes you may be asked to fill in Form IHT200 instead. You will also need Form IHT200 if you discover at the end of your calculations that the estate is liable for inheritance tax.

The main part of the form requires you to list the deceased's assets and put a valuation on them. When you informed the various banks, building societies, insurance and investment companies of the deceased's death they should have given you such information. If not, now is the time to ask them for this.

There is normally no need to bring in a professional valuer to value property unless it is extremely valuable. Instead you could find out how much similar properties in the area have sold for in recent months and base your valuation on this. Local estate agents and the local Land Registry Office can be of help. Note that selling prices are usually lower than asking prices. However, you should beware of grossly undervaluing the property because if you decide to sell it soon after you could incur a large amount of capital gains tax to pay!

After valuing the estate you need to deduct liabilities – which will include funeral expenses and any other payments due. You also need to deduct exemptions, such as the value of the house if it is passing to a joint owner.

If you find after your calculations that the net estate is above the IHT threshold, it might be sensible to see if any adjustments are possible to the figures. Sometimes it is possible to make adjustments legitimately to the will in order to make it more tax efficient, but for this you will need legal advice.

ADMINISTERING THE ESTATE

There are three stages to go through:

◆ collect all the assets

◆ pay the bills and taxes

◆ distribute the net assets.

This may sound like a simple process that can be completed in a day or two, but if some of the assets are in the form of property or goods which have to be sold, or are investments which have a specific maturity date, for example, it can turn out to be a long drawn out affair. Along the way you may discover assets that you were unaware of or unexpected debts that have to be paid.

If you are unable to ascertain from the deceased's records who the creditors are, you may need to advertise in a local newspaper or the *London Gazette*.

It is not unreasonable to allow a period of six months – or even longer – to wind up the estate.

Records need to be kept of all these transactions, and it is also advisable to set up a special executor's bank account for paying in monies received and making out cheques to creditors and beneficiaries (see Figure 16). The tax authorities have the power to do spot checks, and for this reason everything must be accounted for. This means you should obtain receipts from everyone, including those people receiving bequests.

In property transfers it is necessary to register the change of ownership of the property with the Land Registry using Form AS1. This is known as Assent.

Estate of the Late Algernon Snaith

Receipts

05.01.0X	Cash	2000.00
23.02.0X	Reynolds Bank	1000.00
23.02.0X	Hogarth Building Society	2050.00
23.02.0X	Gainsborough PEP	5934.60
24.02.0X	Turner ISA	12421.12
25.02.0X	Hogarth Investment Bond	5698.20
09.03.0X	Income Tax Rebate	420.07
TOTAL RECEIPTS		**£29523.99**

Payments

05.01.0X	Registry Office	16.00
17.01.0X	Probate Office	135.00
19.02.0X	Turner Funeral Service: funeral	2430.00
19.02.0X	Spencer Hotel: funeral reception	200.00
15.03.0X	Sudbury Cemetery: memorial plaque	160.00
19.04.0X	Piper Solicitors: property transfer	415.48
20.04.0X	Sundry executors' expenses	350.00
04.05.0X	Jonathan Snaith: bequest	5000.00
04.05.0X	Orlando Snaith: bequest	5000.00
04.05.0X	Dorothea Snaith: bequest	5000.00
04.05.0X	RSPCA: bequest	500.00
TOTAL PAYMENTS		**19206.48**
Residue payable to Elizabeth Snaith		**10317.51**

Figure 16. Specimen executors' accounts.

Usually a will nominates a person or people to receive the residue of the estate, and they should be provided with a set of accounts to show how the estate has been administered.

6

Coping with Bereavement

The death of a loved one can be disorientating. The longer and closer your relationship with the deceased, the greater will be the sense of loss. But the pain can be just as intense in situations where death occurred unexpectedly, or was of someone in the first blush of youth who has been denied the chance to achieve his or her potential.

This final chapter focuses on those who have suffered a bereavement. Many will be elderly people who have lost a lifelong partner and now face the prospect of living alone. But some will be relatively young: parents who have lost a child through accident or illness; children who have lost one or both of their parents; young people who have lost their best friend or prospective marriage partner.

Whether you are prepared for the death or not, you are bound to be affected in some way when it occurs.

SPENDING TIME WITH THE DYING PERSON

Sudden deaths are the exception, and normally we have plenty of warning that a person is in the final stages of their life. I firmly believe that spending time with people during their last days or weeks is of benefit not only to them, but also to ourselves and our grieving process.

It can be a harrowing experience watching life ebb away, and if someone is confused, unable to communicate or in a coma, you may well wonder whether there is any point in being with them. Yet time spent with a person while they are still alive is more purposeful than time spent thinking about them when they have gone, and during the vigil you gradually become reconciled to their passing.

Very old people often regress into the past and incidents from their childhood suddenly become more vivid to them than the present. Sometimes they may not even recognise you, which can be disconcerting, but this is not a reason to stay away.

A friend of mine flew thousands of miles in order to be at the bedside of a dying parent. His father died three days after his arrival, but any grief he felt was mingled with relief that he had managed to be with him in his final hours. He considered the effort well worth it.

REACTIONS TO DEATH

The death of a close family member or friend can give rise to a number of different feelings, some of which you may have never experienced before and may not know how to cope with. Be assured that you are not the first and only person to have had such feelings, and you may well recognise some of the more common reactions which are listed here.

Anger

Why did this person have to die? Why did this happen to me? This is a common reaction in the case of a death, especially one for which you were unprepared. The anger may be directed at the person who has died for leaving you in the lurch . . . or at yourself for not anticipating it . . . or towards others for their apparent indifference to your feelings. It is a good idea to find a close confidant with whom you can vent your anger rather than make a public display of it.

Anxiety

Anxiety is often triggered by a fear of the unknown, and if you have been close to a person for a period of decades and now find yourself alone, you may start to panic. You wonder what you are going to do and how you are going to manage now that life's certainties are no longer there. Yet people often underestimate their ability to cope with adversity: problems are not insuperable and eventually work themselves out. If not, you should seek advice.

Grief

You are overcome with sorrow and want to shut yourself away and have a good cry. Such feelings occur as you come across objects associated with the deceased, look at photos of them or recall particular events in the past in which they were prominent. A good cry is nothing to be ashamed of and can, in fact, be very therapeutic. The custom of weeping and wailing at a person's burial is quite normal in some cultures, so do not feel you have to bottle up your emotions and maintain a stiff upper lip.

Guilt

Could I have done something to prevent this? Why didn't I spend more time with the deceased while he was still alive? Sometimes people are excessively hard on themselves and blame themselves for the death. By and large these feelings of guilt are misplaced, and the people who feel guilt most accutely are generally those who have made the greatest contribution to the dead person's life.

Helplessness

You feel numb and lifeless and sit around doing nothing; you seem to lack the energy or inclination to do simple routine tasks; you cannot concentrate; nothing seems to matter any more and you feel you want to give up on life. This is where close friends and relations can be a boon and you should welcome any attempts on their part to buck you up and help you regain your confidence to do things.

Impatience

It can take months to sort out the deceased's affairs, and you get annoyed at the amount of bureaucracy you have to wade through and the inordinate amount of time it takes to get even simple things done. It gets even worse if the funeral has to be delayed because of a coroner's investigation. You need to accept that nothing you do can speed things up, and if you can divert your attention to activities over which you have some control, delays will prove less of an irritant.

Loneliness

If you shared much of your life with the deceased – and, more particularly, if you lived together – you will find a yawning gap in your life. The house or flat where you live will feel empty and there are times when you imagine you hear the deceased's voice. To overcome feelings of loneliness you should resolve to get out of the house more and extend your circle of acquaintances. Don't wait for people to come to see you; get out and join them. A pet can be an excellent companion, and if you do not have one, there are thousands of pets in animal shelters up and down the country looking for good homes.

Moodiness

People can experience a wide range of emotions when someone dies and sometimes there are violent mood swings from confidence to despair, from acceptance to bitterness. If you are the sort of person who is accustomed to keeping your feelings under control, these can be disconcerting and you may even wonder if you are losing your grip on reality. Though this is in no sense an abnormal reponse to stress, if you are at all worried you should seek advice from your doctor.

Physical reactions

Headaches, nausea, dizziness, lassitude, sleeplessness, lack of appetite, skin complaints, aches and pains – these are some of the physical effects that can be triggered by the death of a loved one or, indeed, any other unexpected change to one's routine. If your emotional defences are at a low ebb, you may imagine you are suffering from all kinds of illnesses and ailments. Talk matters over with your doctor and he may be able to prescribe suitable remedies. In most cases there is nothing seriously wrong with you and the problems should soon pass.

Shock and denial

You cannot believe that someone close to you has died and you have problems in coming to terms with the death. This is particularly true if you have been living with a person for many years. You may expect the deceased to come walking in through the door at any moment, and it will take a period of readjustment before you come to accept that this will never happen again.

Fortunately some of the feelings experienced are positive ones. Here are a few which bereaved people have mentioned to me.

Gratitude

Sometimes it is not until people die and the tributes flow in that you recognise the contribution they have made to your life and that of so many others. It is then that you experience a feeling of gratitude – even pride – that you have had the privilege of knowing them and that they have lived such a fulfilling life.

Liberation

This may sound a very odd reaction, but there are countless numbers of people who have the responsibility of caring for an elderly or infirm relative or friend – a duty that places ever-increasing demands on one's time and patience. Suddenly the burden is lifted, you are no longer bound to a strict routine and for once you have the luxury of plenty of time to devote to your own interests. You are free.

Relief

One acquaintance of mine recalled how she had wept a lot before her husband died, but hardly at all afterwards. This was not a sign of heartlessness, but seeing her partner decline before her eyes had been a harrowing experience, and she was clearly relieved that his pain and suffering were now at an end. When death brings a release from pain it is truly a blessing.

Acceptance

Some might brand this fatalism, but people with strong religious beliefs often adopt a more measured response to death, accepting it as part of the natural order of things. Their acceptance is strengthened by the conviction that death is not the end, and that the deceased has now passed on to a better and kinder world.

DELAYED SHOCK

One fairly young widow admits that she did not experience any particular upset after the sudden and untimely death of her husband. But then she had plenty of other matters to occupy her attention: she had two children to look after and much of her effort had to be directed to ensuring that the family had a roof over their head. It was not until a year later that the shock really hit home.

THE GRIEVING PROCESS

When a person dies, some cultures prescribe a period of mourning, as did our Victorian ancestors. The practice of wearing black for a certain period after a death is still practised in parts of the world where it is also common for close friends and relations to maintain a vigil by the coffin of the deceased. This tradition still holds when a prominent figure dies in the UK: the coffin is placed in a public setting for people to pass by and pay their respects.

Such practices are not just for show, but actually help with the grieving process by helping people to come to terms gradually with a person's decease. It is a pity in some ways that in fast-moving Western societies traditions of this kind have fallen into abeyance. As a result there are fewer opportunities to grieve in the company of others.

The funeral

The tradition of elderly people wanting a decent funeral lingers on into this century, which may well explain the popularity of funeral plans. There is much to be said in favour of this idea, even if the person has only limited means.

Although a minority would consider an elaborate funeral a waste of time and money it serves two useful functions: it marks one of the three most important events in life (the others are birth and marriage) and offers consolation to the living. It is one of the principal pillars in the grieving process and, unless there is to be a separate thanksgiving service, represents the only opportunity for people to come together and pay their respects communally.

However, people come to funerals not only out of respect for the dead, but in order to have their spirits lifted. If it is a low key affair they may go away feeling disappointed.

A reception after the formalities are over can be viewed as an integral part of the ceremony offering the chance for relations and friends of the deceased to meet up again – often after a period of several years. The whole occasion represents the start of the healing process.

Memorials to the deceased

One way of coming to terms with a death is to have a memorial to the deceased – in the form of a gravestone, a plaque in a local cemetery, and an entry in the Book of Remembrance at the Cemetery. If there is to be a gravestone, the process of choosing a moumental mason and discussing the wording and design of the memorial can be very consoling. In the case of a plaque, which is usually made by the cemetery itself, only a few words are possible so your options are more limited.

Another popular idea is to plant a tree in a park in the person's memory, or provide a public bench on which his or her name is inscribed.

All of these represent a place associated with the deceased which you can visit at times when you particularly wish to remember them – on their birthday, at Christmas or on the anniversary of their death. Friends and relations who may have been prevented from attending the funeral are thus able to pay their respects at the deceased's final resting place.

Another idea is to have a living memorial – something that lives on after a person's death. One widow I know sponsors an annual concert in her husband's memory. A couple whose daughter died tragically during a gap year overseas built an accommodation block in her memory at an orphanage where she had worked. A widower whose young wife had died of Hodgkinson's disease founded a small charity which supports research into this illness.

The gesture does not have to be elaborate or costly. A donation of books to a library, or the provision of an annual prize for an arts or sports competition, would help keep alive the memory of a loved one. In the case of a pet you can place a tribute on the Blue Cross and other websites. (See Pet Bereavement Support Service.)

Messages of condolence

Once news of the death spreads around, messages of condolence and sympathy cards begin to arrive. Some messages are brief, while others may be fulsome tributes to the dead person. Every one, however, contributes to the grieving process by showing that people care and share your affection for the individual concerned.

It is a good idea to display the cards for a period of time and keep the messages for inspection by anyone who visits. Looking at the cards and reading the messages can be a great consolation to those who knew the person well.

Is a response needed to these messages? No, but it can be beneficial to both sender and recipient to send a brief thank you (see Figure 17) or put a notice to this effect in a newspaper. After my mother's funeral I was happy to send copies of the funeral service to those who sent letters and cards but were unable to attend the service.

---

8 Willow Road
Swallowdale

20 April 200X

Dear Andrew,

Thank you very much for your letter of condolence following the death of your Uncle Robert.

There is no need to apologise for not attending the funeral. You live such a long way from Swallowdale and I know you are particularly busy these days.

I am glad to say that the funeral went off very well and it was a pleasure to see so many relations and old friends of your uncle whom I haven't set eyes on for years.

Thank you for your kind remarks, Yes, he was a very kind and caring man and we shall treasure many happy memories of him.

If you find yourself in this neck of the woods, please drop in for a cup of tea, as I am sure we have a lot to discuss.

Regards

Auntie May

Figure 17. Reply to letter of condolence.

SOURCES OF HELP IN BEREAVEMENT

Your immediate family and friends will doubtless rally round to comfort you in your loss, but if they live far away, or are few and far between, you may start to feel very isolated. However there are many organisations which can provide support in the form of advice, befriending, counselling and self-help during what could be a prolonged period of readjustment.

Many local authorities have bereavement support services operating within their social service departments, but there are also a number of voluntary organisations you could turn to. Some of these are linked to religious groups such as the Jewish Bereavement Counselling Service, the National Islamic Helpline and the Muslim Women's Helpline, while others have no religious affiliations. In many cases the people with whom you are dealing have been through exactly the same experiences that you have and know exactly how you feel.

Cruse

One of the leaders in this field is Cruse Bereavement Care, a charity with 180 branches nationwide which can provide support for anyone who has been bereaved regardless of age, race or belief. The organisation produces a number of helpful leaflets, such as *After the Death of Someone Very Close*. It also has a junior section, RD4U, which offers support to children who have suffered the loss of a parent, friend or relation.

Support for loss of a partner

The National Association of Widows offers a network of local branches offering support to married widows, as well as unmarried women whose partner has died.

Another charity, the Way Foundation, focuses on widows and widowers under the age of 50, of whom there are over 140,000 in Britain.

For those whose husbands have died on active service, whether in war or peacetime, the War Widows Association can offer support. Support is also available for service families through the Soldiers, Sailors, Airmen and Families Association (SSAFA) Forces Help and the British Legion.

The Cruse booklet *Coming Through* will be of help.

Support for loss of a child

The death of a child can be a heart-rending experience and there are a number of specialist organisations offering support to bereaved parents and their families, such as Compassionate Friends, whose affiliate, Support in Bereavement for Brothers and Sisters (SIBBS), supports children who have lost a brother or sister. The Child Bereavement Trust performs a similar function, and the Child Death Helpline operated from Great Ormond Street and Alderhay hospitals is another source of advice and help.

The Foundation for the Study of Cot Deaths has a helpline and network of befrienders for the bereaved, as does the Stillbirth and Neonatal Death Society (SANDS).

For those whose children have met violent deaths, the Families of Murdered Children Association should be your first port of call.

Other support agencies

◆ Lesbians and gays are catered for by the Lesbian and Gay Bereavement Project, and there are a number of organisations which offer more specialist help.

◆ Survivors of Bereavement by Suicide (SOBS) works with those who have been bereaved by suicide.

◆ Support after Murder and Manslaughter (SAMM) provides support for those who have lost a member of their family through murder or manslaughter.

◆ The Sudden Death Support Association counsels those who have suffered a sudden and unexpected death. Incidentally, when a violent death has occurred the police may well assign a police welfare officer to the bereaved family to offer support and advice.

◆ The charity RoadPeace, in addition to campaigning for safer roads, provides support for those who have lost loved ones in road accidents and also erects memorials by roads where deaths have occurred.

◆ Bereavement support is also available from a number of charities which specialise in particular illnesses, such as the British Association of Cancer United Patients.

◆ The death of a pet can cause as much grief as the death of a person, and fortunately help is available from the Pet Bereavement Support Service – a joint venture between the Blue Cross and the Society for Companion Animal Studies.

You will find details of these organisations in the Useful Addresses section of this book. Please bear in mind that this list is by no means comprehensive and you may well be steered towards other organisations (some serving a particular locality) by your doctor, community nurse or local Community Health Council. If you feel particularly desperate, you should call the Samaritans.

I accept that one-to-one counselling may not be the right solution for everyone and you may find that periods of solitude act as the best healer. In the *Bibliography* you will find a selection of books on bereavement which may well give you the solace you require.

LOOKING TO THE FUTURE

'Do not grieve for me when I am gone,' wrote the poet Christina Rossetti, and this is excellent advice. Eventually the grieving has to stop and you have to break loose from the past, particularly if you now find yourself alone. If you were very close to the deceased your sense of loss will not go away easily, but you have to embrace the future no matter how old you may be or feel.

Death, like marriage, is a life-changing event which can open up new vistas and push you in new directions – into the unknown. The initial reaction may be to retreat into your shell; you feel life is hardly worth living and you need a lot of convincing that it has anything to offer you.

Here are a few suggestions for you to consider.

Move out

If you lived under the same roof as the deceased, the property will now seem larger and you may wonder if the time has now come for you to move into smaller and more compact accommodation. It could also hold so many poignant memories that they weigh down on you and you feel you need to escape.

Sometimes the decision is made for you. The house or flat may have to be sold or divided up according to the terms of the will. If the accommodation is rented you may have little option but to move out, as might be the case if the rental agreement is not in your name.

If the choice is up to you, you should not rush into hasty decisions. Selling a property and moving to new accommodation can be a tedious and lengthy process, and having experienced so much disruption in your life in recent weeks, you would be wise to pause before hurling yourself once more into the fray.

After a period of reflection – say, six months to a year – you will have a much clearer picture of how you stand and the options available to you – one of which could well be to stay put.

Get out and meet people

Laugh and the world laughs with you; weep and you weep alone. It is important for you to get out and about rather than expect people to visit you. Some will mistakenly believe that you prefer to be left alone to grieve and feel awkward about approaching you. By getting out you will be sending out a signal that you wish to have company.

This chapter has listed a number of organisations which offer support to the bereaved. However, many of them go much further than that and offer you the opportunity to develop friendships with people who share similar experiences to you and would welcome your company.

Elderly people will find there are social clubs in their area which meet regularly for tea or lunch. Age Concern and Help the Aged can provide details of these. Community Health Councils and religious organisations are other good sources of information.

Develop new interests

If you have devoted a great deal of your time to looking after the person now deceased, you will eventually find that time hangs heavy. Now is the time to fill your newly acquired leisure time by taking up a new hobby, perhaps, or attending a course in a subject that interests you. Some bereaved people try to develop practical skills, such as cookery and financial management, which will enable them to cope better.

Local FE colleges and adult education centres normally have a broad range of study courses on offer, as do the Workers' Educational Association and university continuing education departments whose brochures appear in public libraries around August and September. A course in an adult residential college is also an option, and if you require something more challenging you could enrol with the Open University.

An important result of attending courses like these is that you meet people, and the intellectual effort involved helps to stimulate the brain and chase away any brooding on the past. Although you may find study something of a struggle in the early stages, after a time you will find that the effort is worth it.

You will find addresses for these organisations in the *Useful Addresses* section.

Going on holiday

After a gruelling period of weeks and months getting things sorted, why not get away for a while? If friends and relations invite you to stay with them, you should jump at the chance. If the weather is foul and depressing, why not book yourself a holiday in the sun?

You may hesitate to do this, and certainly if you and the deceased have been used to holidaying together, it may require a little courage to go off on your own. One solution is to look around for friends or relations who are in a similar position and might be only too happy to go off on holiday with you.

If you feel you could manage alone, you could investigate some of the holiday companies which specialise in holidays for people who are single – or, if you have children, for single parents. However, don't assume that all other travel firms cater solely for couples and families; many unattached people take such holidays and make friends as they go along. Cruises seem to provide a particularly good opportunity to meet others, as do study tours and adventure holidays, though the latter tend to be for the young and intrepid.

Holidays can have a therapeutic effect: they help you to put the recent past behind you and to recharge your batteries. Away from your normal surroundings you have an opportunity to think things over at leisure and consider what shape your future might take.

Going on Holiday, a factsheet published by Cruse Bereavement Care, offers some useful tips.

Find a new outlet for your energies

Although many of the people who have the greatest difficulty in coming to terms with bereavement are aged 60 plus, a substantial minority are not. They are the children, siblings, parents or friends of the deceased and will range from the very young to people in the prime of life.

Most will decide to carry on as normal; they may even start to put more effort into their work or study in a bid to shake off memories of the past. Others may feel the need to begin afresh and try a new job, a new career or some other new activity.

The way forward could be linked in some way to the person you have lost. Two parents whose daughter died of drug abuse began a campaign to warn other young people of the dangers of taking harmful substances. Another couple set up a small charity to improve facilities for profoundly disabled children as a result of their experiences.

You may prefer to work with institutions which are already functioning: helping out at a local hospice or offering support to victims of crime are just two examples of useful work you can do. If you now have fewer ties to hold you back, you could look into the possibility of getting a job abroad – as a volunteer in developing countries, perhaps.

Death is the end of one life, but it may well prove a turning point in the lives of those who live on. In the light of your new circumstances you should be prepared to re-examine your goals and embrace new challenges. Good luck!

7

A Final Word

A headmaster once affirmed that the aim of his school was to equip his students for life. 'How fascinating,' was the reaction of Father Paul Nevill, a former headmaster of a famous Catholic public school. 'You see at Ampleforth we always seek to prepare our boys for death.'

The purpose of this handbook could be regarded as preparation for death, too, though perhaps not in the same sense that Father Nevill meant it. Death is not a matter we can sweep under the carpet, and if we face up to it and its various ramifications, we will surely be better equipped to cope when it occurs.

When I began writing this book I was coy about mentioning the subject of my project to others for fear it might prove a conversation-stopper. I could not have been more wrong. People were only too ready to open up and share their experiences with me – not out of morbid interest, but because they welcomed the opportunity to talk about a difficult subject that is too often avoided.

Of course, discussing death over lunch or at a cocktail party is a very different matter from talking about it to someone who has just been diagnosed with an incurable cancer or who has lost a bosom pal in tragic circumstances. When death becomes reality, words do not flow easily, and it requires courage on the part of everybody concerned to grasp the nettle and plan ahead.

However, avoiding the subject entirely or speaking about it in hushed whispers is unlikely to lessen the pain and the shock. It is better by far to accept the inevitable and devote time to finding practical solutions which will ensure that life goes on after one of our number makes an exit.

This book has been a cursory survey of the issues to be considered as death approaches and after it has occurred. While the broad brush approach will have sufficed for many readers, there will be some who need to explore some of the issues in greater detail, and for these I have included a select list of addresses and books which can provide further information and help.

Appendix A

Bibliography

HANDBOOKS ON DEATH AND FUNERALS

A Practical Guide to Alternative Funerals Kate Gordon (Constable & Robinson).

Complete Book of Funeral Planning, Readings and Music R. Johnstone-Burt (Foulsham).

Daily Telegraph Guide to Funerals and Bereavement Sam Weller (Kogan Page).

The Dead Good Funerals Book Sue Gill and John Fox (Engineers of the Imagination).

The Funeral Handbook Giles Legood and Ian Markham (SPCK).

Funerals: A Practical Guide to the New Services R. Anne Horton (Church House Publishing).

Funerals without God Jane Wynne Willson (Prometheus Books).

How to Arrange a Funeral Toby Walne (Age Concern).

In Your Own Time: Guide for Patients and Carers facing a Last Illness at Home Elizabeth Lee (OUP).

The Natural Death Handbook Stephanie Wienrich, editor (Cygnus Books).

Well Chosen Words: How to Write a Eulogy (Co-operative Funeralcare). This can be downloaded from www. funeralcare.co-op.co.uk.

LEGAL HANDBOOKS

Do It Yourself Last Will and Testament (Law Pack).

Elite Last Will and Testament Do It Yourself Pack (Elite Personnel Management Ltd).

How to Deal with Death and Probate Gordon Bowley (How To Books)

How to Write your Will Marlene Garsia (Kogan Page).

Make Your own Will: The Plain English Guide to Making a Will A. K. Biggs (Jordan Publishing).

Making a Will: A Self-Help Guide Gordon Bowley (How To Books).

Making Your Will: Action Pack (Which? Books).

Probate Guide Gill Cockburn (ed) (Law Pack).

What to do After a Death in England and Wales (Department for Work and Pensions).

Wills and Probate Paul Elmhirst (Which? Books).

Wills and Probate Jacqueline Martin and Richard Pooley (Teach Yourself Books).

Wills, Power of Attorney and Probate Guide (Lawpack Publishing).

Wills, Probate and Inheritance Tax for Dummies Julian Knight (John Wiley and Sons).

COLLECTIONS OF PROSE AND POETRY SUITABLE FOR FUNERALS

At the End is Harvest Agnes Whitaker (Darton, Longman & Todd).

Do Not Go Gentle: Funeral Poems Neil Astley, editor (Bloodaxe Books).

Funerals: An Anthology and Guide Andrew Best, James
Bentley and Jackie Hunt, editors (Hodder & Stoughton).

In Loving Memory: A Collection of Memorial Resources Sally
Emerson, editor (Little Brown).

One Hundred Readings for Bereavement Robert Atwell, editor
(Canterbury Press).

Poems and Readings for Funerals Julia Watson, compiler
(Penguin).

Remember: One Hundred Readings on Loss Robert Atwell
(Canterbury Press).

Seasons of Life Nigel Collins, editor (Rationalist Press
Association). Readings expressing a Humanist outlook.

The Long Pale Corridor Judi Benson and Agneta Falk, editors
(Bloodaxe Books).

BOOKS ON BEREAVEMENT

A Guide to Handling Bereavement Adrian Lewis
(Straightforward Publishing).

A Grief Observed C. S. Lewis (Faber & Faber).

A Voice for Those Bereaved by Suicide Sarah McCarthy
(Veritas).

And When Did You Last See Your Father? Blake Morrison
(Granta).

Bereaved by Suicide Patrick Shannon (Cruse Bereavement Care).

Bereavement: Your Questions Answered Ursula Markham
(Element).

Can I Let You Go, My Love? Kay van Dijk (Acorn).

Cold Comfort: Stories of Death and Bereavement James
Loader, editor (Serpent's Tale).

Coping with Bereavement Hamish McIlwraith (Oneworld Publications).

Death and Bereavement Across Cultures Colin Murray Parkes (Routledge).

Diary of a Grief Peter Woods (William Sessions).

Facing Grief: Bereavement and the Young Adult Susan Wallbank (Lutterworth Press).

How to Survive Bereavement Andrea Kon (Help Yourself!).

Living with Bereavement Alex James (Elliot Right Way Books).

Living with Grief Tony Lake (Sheldon).

Living with Loss: A Book for the Widowed Liz McNeill Taylor (Constable & Robinson).

My Father Died: A Booklet for Young People Susan Wallbank (Cruse Bereavement Care).

My Mother Died: A Booklet for Young People Susan Wallbank (Cruse Bereavement Care).

Past Caring: The Beginning, Not the End Audrey Jenkinson (Polperro Heritage Press).

Sibling Bereavement Ann Farrant (Continuum).

Staying Close: A Positive Approach to Dying and Bereavement Michael Waterhouse (Constable & Robinson).

The Bereaved Parent Harriet Sarnoff Schiff (Souvenir Press).

The Courage to Grieve Judy Tatelbaum (Heinemann).

The Tibetan Book of Living and Dying Sogyal Rinpoche (Rider & Co).

Through Grief: A Bereavement Journey Elizabeth Collick (Darton, Longman & Todd).

Time to Grieve Michael Dunn (How To Books).

When Goodbye is Forever Lois Rock (Lion Hudson).

When Parents Die Rebecca Abrams (Routledge).

When the Crying's Done: A Journey Through Widowhood Jeannette Kupfermann (Robson).

When Your Parent Dies: Insights for Bereaved Adults Caroline Morcom (Cruse Bereavement Care).

Widow's Journey: A Return to Living Xenia Rose (Souvenir Press).

You'll Get Over It: Rage of Bereavement Virginia Ironside (Hamish Hamilton).

Appendix B

USEFUL ADDRESSES

ASSOCIATIONS

Advice Services Alliance
Bramah House
65–71 Bermondsey Street
London SE1 3XF
www.advicenow.org.uk
Co-ordinating body for UK advice centres including Citizens'
  Advice Bureau, Age Concern

Age Concern England
Astral House
1268 London Road
Norbury
London SW16 4ER
Telephone: 0800 009966
Website: www.ageconcern.org.uk

Age Concern Northern Ireland
3 Lower Crescent
Belfast BT7 1NR
Telephone: 02690 245729
Website: www.ageconcernni.org

Age Concern Scotland
Leonard Small House
113 Rose Street
Edinburgh EH2 3DT
Telephone: 0131 220 3345
Website: www.ageconcernscotland.org.uk

Age Concern Wales
4th Floor
1 Cathedral Road
Cardiff CF11 9SD
Telephone: 02920 371566
Website: www.accymru.org.uk

Bereavement Register
Freepost SEA 8240
Sevenoaks TN13 1YR
Telephone: 08706 007222
Website: www.the-bereavement-register.org.uk

British Humanist Association
1 Gower Street
London WC1E 6HD
Telephone: 020 7079 3580
www.humanism.org.uk

British Organ Donor Society (BODY)
Baldsham
Cambridge CB1 6DL
Telephone: 01223 893636
Website: www.body.orpheusweb.co.uk

Carers UK
20–25 Glasshouse Yard
London EC1A 4JT
Telephone: 020 7490 8818
Website: www.carersuk.org

Child Bereavement Trust
Aston House
West Wycombe
Bucks HP14 3AG
Telephone: 0845 357 1000
Website: www.childbereavement.org.uk

Citizens' Advice Bureau
Look in local telephone directory
Website: www.citizensadvice.org.uk

Cremation Society of Great Britain
2nd Floor
Brecon House
16 Albion Place
Maidstone ME14 5DZ
Telephone: 01622 688292
Website: www.cremation.org.uk

Help the Aged
207–221 Pentonville Road
London N1 9UZ
Telephone: 020 7278 1114
Website: www.helptheaged.org.uk

Hospice Information Service
St Christopher's Hospice
51–59 Lawrie Park Road
Sydenham
London SE26 6DZ
Telephone: 0870 903 3903
Website: www.hospiceinformation.info

Humanist Society of Scotland
20 Inverkeith Row
Edinburgh EH3 5QH
Website: www.humanism-scotland.org.uk

INQUEST
89–93 Fonthill Road
London N4 2JH
Telephone: 020 7263 1111
Website: www.inquest.org.uk
Help and advice where a coroner's inquest has to be held.

Institute of Professional Willwriters
Trinity Point
New Road
Halesowen B63 3HY
Website: www.ipw.org.uk
Telephone: 0845 644 2042

Jewish Bereavement Counselling Service
8/10 Forty Avenue
Wembley HA9 8JW

Telephone: 020 8385 1874

Website: www.jvisit.org.uk

Law Society of England & Wales

113 Chancery Lane

London WC2A 1PL

Telephone: 020 7242 1222

Website: www.lawsociety.org.uk and www.solicitors-online.com

Law Society of Northern Ireland

98 Victoria Street

Belfast BT1 3JZ

Telephone: 02890 231614

Website: www.lawsoc-ni.org

Law Society of Scotland

26 Drumsheigh Gardens

Edinburgh EH3 7YR

Telephone: 0131 226 7411

Website: www.lawscot.org.uk

National Association of Widows

48 Queens Road

Coventry CV1 3ER

Telephone: 0845 8382261

Website: www.nawidows.org.uk

National Institute for Adult Continuing Education

20 Princess Road West

Leicester LE1 6TP

Telephone: 0116 204 4200

Website: www.niace.org.uk

National Secular Society
25 Red Lion Square
London WC1R 4RL
Telephone: 020 7404 3126
Website: www.secularism.org.uk

National Society of Allied and Independent Funeral
  Directors
3 Bullfields
Sawbridgeworth
Herts CM21 9DB
Telephone: 0845 230 6777
Website: www.saif.org.uk

National Will Register
Willdata
King's Business Park
King's Yard
Fordingbridge
Hants SP6 1AB
Telephone: 0845 009 7000
Website: www.willdata.info

Natural Death Centre
6 Blackstock Mews
Blackstock Road
London N4 2BT
Telephone: 0871 288 2098
Website: www.naturaldeath.org.uk

Next of Kin International
Abacus House
Dudley Street
Luton LU2 0BR
Website: www.nextofkin.org.uk and www.nextofkin.com

The Open University
PO Box 724
Walton Hall
Milton Keynes MK7 6ZS
Telephone: 01908 653231
Website: www.open.ac.uk

Voluntary Euthanasia Society
13 Prince of Wales Terrace
London W8 5PG
Telephone: 0870 777 7868
Website: www.dignityindying.org.uk

Will Registry Office
5 High Street
Maidenhead
Berks SL6 1JA
Website: www.thewillregistryoffice.co.uk

Workers' Educational Association
Quick House
65 Clifton Street
London EC4A 4JE
Telephone: 020 7426 3450
Website: www.wea.org.uk

BEREAVEMENT SERVICES

British Association of Cancer United Patients
3 Bath Place
Rivington Street
London EC2A 3JR
Telephone: 0808 800 1234
Website: www.cancerbacup.org.uk

Child Death Helpline
Telephone: 0800 282986

Cruse Bereavement Care
Cruse House
126 Sheen Road
Richmond
Surrey TW9 1UR
Telephone: 0870 167 1677
Cruse Youthline: 0808 808 1677
Website: www.cruse.org.uk

Families of Murdered Children
Helpline: 01698 336646; 07775 626779
Website: www.fomc.org.uk

Foundation for the Study of Infant Deaths
Artillery House
11–19 Artillery Row
London SW1P 1RT
Telephone: 020 7233 2090
Website: www.sids.org.uk/fsid

Lesbian and Gay Bereavement Project
THT Counselling
111–117 Lancaster Road
London W11 1QT
Telephone: 020 8455 8894
Website: www.tht.org.uk

Pet Bereavement Support Service
The Blue Cross
Shilton Road
Burford OX18 4PF
Telephone: 0800 096 6606
Website: www.bluecross.org.uk

RD4U
Youth Involvement Project
Cruse Bereavement Care
Central Hall
Oldham Street
Manchester M1 1JT
Helpline: 0808 808 1677
Website: www.rd4u.org.uk

RoadPeace
PO Box 2579
London NW10 3PW
Helpline: 08454 500355
Website: www.roadpeace.org

The Samaritans
Telephone: 0845 790 9090
Website: www.samaritans.org.uk

SIBBS (see Compassionate Friends)

SSAFA Forces Help
19 Queen Elizabeth Street
London SE1 2LP
Telephone: 0845 1300 975
Website: www.ssafa.org.uk

Stillbirth and Neonatal Death Society
28 Portland Place
London W1N 4DE
Telephone: 020 7436 5881
Website: www.uk-sands.org

Sudden Death Support Association
Eldon House
The Street
Eversley
Hook
Hants RG27 0PJ
Telephone: 01189 733 939
Website: www.patient.co.uk/showdoc

Support After Murder and Manslaughter
Cranmer House
39 Brixton Road
London SW9 6DZ
Telephone: 020 7735 3838
Website: www.samm.org.uk

Survivors of Bereavement by Suicide (SOBS)
Volserve House

14–18 West Bar Green
Sheffield S1 2DA
Telephone: 0870 241 3337
Website: www.uk-sobs.org.uk

The Compassionate Friends
53 North Street
Bristol BS3 1EN
Telephone: 0117 914 0630
Website: www.tcf.org.uk
For families which have lost a child

War Widows Association
48 Pall Mall
London SW1Y 5JY
Telephone: 0870 241 1305
Website: www.warwidowsassociation.org.uk

The Way Foundation
PO Box 6767
Brackley NN13 6YW
Telephone: 0870 011 3450
Website: www.wayfoundation.org.uk
For younger widows and widowers

FUNERALS AND FUNERAL PLANS
Age Concern Funeral Plan
Telephone: 0800 731 0651

Co-operative Funeral Plan Service
8th Floor
Trafford Plaza

PO Box 183
73 Seymour Grove
Manchester M16 0SQ
Website: www.co-operativefuneralcare.co.uk

Funeral Planning Authority
Knellstone House
Udimore
Rye TN31 6AR
Telephone: 0845 601 9619
Website: www.funeralplanningauthority.com

Funeral Plans UK
8 Copperfields
Chew Moor
Bolton BL6 4HZ
Telephone: 01942 799810
Website: www.funeral-plans-uk.co.uk

Golden Charter Funeral Plan
Melville House
70 Drymen Road
Glasgow G61 2RP
Telephone: 0800 833800
Website: www.goldencharter.com

Golden Leaves Funeral Plan
299–305 Whitehorse Road
Croydon CR0 2HR
Telephone: 0800 854448
Website: www.goldenleaves.co.uk

Help the Aged Funeral Plan
Telephone: 0800 169 1112

National Association of Funeral Directors
618 Warwick Road
Solihull
West Midlands B91 1AA
Telephone: 0845 230 1343; 0121 711 1343
Website: www.nafd.org.uk

National Association for Pre-paid Funeral Plans
15 Riverside Drive
Solihull B91 3HH
Telephone: 0121 705 5133
Website: www.napfp.co.uk

National Society of Allied and Independent Funeral
   Directors
3 Bullfields
Sawbridgeworth
Herts CM21 9DB
Telephone: 0845 230 6777
Website: www.saif.org.uk

A number of funeral directors offer their own funeral plans,
notably Co-operative Funeralcare and Dignity.

GOVERNMENT OFFICES AND AGENCIES

Department of Work and Pensions
Contact local Social Security or Job Centre Office.

General Register Office
Southport
Merseyside PR8 2LD
Telephone: 0845 603 7788
Website: www.gro.gov.uk

General Register Office
Overseas Section
Smedley Hydro
Trafalgar Road
Birkdale
Southport PR8 2HH
Telephone: 0151 471 4801
Website: www.gro.gov.uk

General Register Office for Northern Ireland
Oxford House
49 Chichester Street
Belfast BT1 4HL
Telephone: 028 9027 0274
Website: www.belfastcity.gov.uk

General Register Office for Scotland
New Register House
3 West Register Street
Edinburgh EH1 3YT
Telephone: 0131 334 0380
Wesbite: www.gro-scotland.gov.uk

HM Inspector of Anatomy
Room 630
Department of Health
Wellington House
153 Waterloo Road
London SE1 8UG
Telephone: 020 7972 4551

HM Revenue and Customs
See telephone directory for local Inland Revenue Office

HM Revenue and Customs
IR Capital Tax Office (for IHT)
Ferrers House
PO Box 38
Castle Meadow Road
Nottingham NG2 1BB
Website: www.hmrc.gov.uk/cto
(Offices in Edinburgh and Belfast)

Land Registry
See local telephone directory for details
Website: www.landregisteronline.co.uk

NHS Blood and Transplant
Fox Den Road
Stoke Gifford
Bristol BS34 8RR
Telephone: 0845 606 0400; 0117 975 7575
Website: www.uktransplant.org.uk

Passport Office
Telephone: 0870 521 0410
Website: www.passport.gov.uk

The Pension Service
Telephone: 0845 606 0265
www.thepensionservice.gov.uk

Principal Probate Registry
The Court Service
42–49 High Holborn
London WC1N 6NP
Probate and Inheritance Tax: 0845 302 0900
Website: www.courtservice.gov.uk

Public Guardianship Office
Archway Tower
2 Junction Road
London N19 5SZ
Telephone: 020 7664 7327
Website: www.guardianship.gov.uk

Index

If you want to know how ... to write your own life story

'The emphasis is not to write a bestseller, but a personal record for family and friends to enjoy. Whilst those with higher ambitions will find the book helpful, it is essentially intended for the enthusiastic hobbyist writing to celebrate life. Typically this will include those you have known and loved, the events that have shaped your life and the fascinating social history witnessed along the way. Use this book as it suits you. Select what you want and let the memories roll!'

Michael Oke

Times of Our Lives

The essential companion for writing your own life story
Michael Oke

'. . . an invaluable source of inspiration and guidance to get the task started – and completed!' – *Best of British*

'Surprise yourself as you unlock hundreds of memories of yesteryear. Whether you are looking to write your life story, or simply enjoy reminiscing, you will be amazed at what you remember with the help of this book.' – *The Daily Telegraph*

'This is *the* essential companion for writing your own life story.' – *Yours*
ISBN 1 85703 970 X

If you want to know how . . . to keep your home and your family safe from crime

'There is a lot that the average person can do to protect themselves, their family and their property. This book will teach you how to perform a security review on your home and show you what countermeasures you can take to ensure that you are *highly unlikely* to be a victim of crime.'

Des Conway

The Home Security Handbook

How to keep your home and family safe from crime
D. G. Conway

Surveys have revealed that when asked what people worry most about for themselves and their family 45% of them said 'CRIME'. Crime statistics certainly indicate that people have good reason to worry: A burglary takes place on average every 30 seconds in the UK.

Alarming though this and other statistics may be, this book will show you how you can use them to reduce the risk of becoming a crime statistic yourself. It will teach you how to audit and review your home and lifestyle, to identify a range of vulnerabilities, threats and risks and then show you how to provide effective countermeasures to avoid the threat and reduce the risk.

The countermeasures suggested are designed to be realistic, achievable at minimal cost and effort and simple enough to be introduced or implemented by the average person.

Des Conway has over 20 years security experience, which combines police service with commercial security consultancy. He has experienced countless security reviews of domestic and commercial properties, delivering reports highlighting vulnerabilities, and recommending simple, affordable and achievable countermeasures.

ISBN 1 84528 024 5

If you want to know how . . . to find out more about our greatest writers

'We have in the British Isles a wonderfully rich store of literature. The purpose of this book is to offer a guide to that inheritance and to invite exploration of the great writers. You will find help towards understanding each writer's work, key biographical detail, extracts from the literature, and suggestions for further reading. The body of our literature is not a territory that we need feel obliged to map out in systematic and comprehensive detail. We can enjoy it inconsequentially, dipping into its random pleasures. I hope this book will encourage that.'

John Carrington

Our Greatest Writers
and their major works
John Carrington

'A perfect tool for upping your literary IQ.' – *The Good Book Guide*

'Excellent.' – *The Teacher*

This book will take you to the heart of the great literature of the English language, to discover or rediscover the best that has been written. In concise and clearly structured sections, all the major writers are presented in order of their birth, giving a strong sense of the unfolding history of English literature from *Beowulf* to Seamus Heaney.

ISBN 1 84528 037 7

How To Books are available through all good bookshops, or you can order direct from us through Grantham Book Services.

Tel: +44 (0)1476 541080
Fax: +44 (0)1476 541061
Email: orders@gbs.tbs-ltd.co.uk

Or via our website

www.howtobooks.co.uk

To order via any of these methods please quote the title(s) of the book(s) and your credit card number together with its expiry date.

For further information about our books and catalogue, please contact:

How To Books
Spring Hill House
Spring Hill Road
Begbroke
Oxford OX5 1RX
Visit our web site at

www.howtobooks.co.uk

Or you can contact us by email at info@howtobooks.co.uk